A Virtue Epistemology

A Virtue Epistemology

Apt Belief and Reflective Knowledge, Volume I

Ernest Sosa

CLARENDON PRESS · OXFORD

OXFORD

UNIVERSITY PRESS

Great Clarendon Street, Oxford OX2 6DP

Oxford University Press is a department of the University of Oxford.
It furthers the University's objective of excellence in research, scholarship,
and education by publishing worldwide in

Oxford New York

Auckland Cape Town Dar es Salaam Hong Kong Karachi
Kuala Lumpur Madrid Melbourne Mexico City Nairobi
New Delhi Shanghai Taipei Toronto

With offices in

Argentina Austria Brazil Chile Czech Republic France Greece
Guatemala Hungary Italy Japan Poland Portugal Singapore
South Korea Switzerland Thailand Turkey Ukraine Vietnam

Oxford is a registered trade mark of Oxford University Press
in the UK and in certain other countries

Published in the United States
by Oxford University Press Inc., New York

British Library Cataloguing in Publication Data

Data available

Library of Congress Cataloging in Publication Data

Data available

ISBN 978-0-19-929702-3

10 9 8 7 6 5 4 3 2 1

Typeset by Laserwords Private Limited, Chennai, India
Printed in Great Britain
on acid-free paper by
Biddles Ltd., King's Lynn, Norfolk

For David

Contents

Preface to the Two-Volume Work

The first of these two volumes is described in its preface below. The second volume will draw together my widely scattered but mutually supportive responses to the problems of epistemic circularity. Its contents will be described in its own preface.

My debts in epistemology are many and varied, and span a long, still lengthening career. I have learned from the field's main contributors, whose names make up a long list. Many of them contributed to *Ernest Sosa and His Critics*, much to my benefit, for which I am deeply grateful. For close and sustained discussion of epistemology over many years, in numerous conversations, in private and public settings, three people stand out: John Greco, Peter Klein, and David Sosa.

Ramon Lemos was my main undergraduate teacher; I am grateful for his influence. Nicholas Rescher and Wilfrid Sellars, early graduate teachers, had their main influence through their writings. Roderick Chisholm, never my formal teacher, was my main teacher in fact: teacher, colleague, and collaborator for decades, with a pervasive influence. Immediate colleagues with whom I have discussed epistemology helpfully in joint seminars, include Rob Bolton, Jaegwon Kim, Brian McLaughlin, and, especially, Alvin Goldman, Peter Klein, and Jim Van Cleve.

Epistemology students in recent years have also helped me to see things more clearly and to explain them better:

Juan Comesaña, Derek Ettinger, Jeremy Fantl, Carl Feier-abend Ben Fiedor, Brie Gertler, Stephen Grimm, Allan Hazlett, Robert Howell, Jonathan Ichikawa, Alex Jackson, Jason Kawall, Chris Knapp, Jennifer Lackey, Peter Marton, David Matheson, Douglas McDermid, Matt McGrath, Josh Orozco, Michael Pace, Baron Reed, Joseph Shieber, Jerry Steinhofer, John Turri, and Stephanie Wykstra. The epistemology dissertation workshops that I have run for many years, composed of many of these students, have been at least as instructive to me as I hope to them.

Preface and Acknowledgments

Here are the six Locke Lectures given in Oxford in May and June of 2005.[1] Published now very nearly as delivered, they argue for two levels of knowledge, the animal and the reflective, each viewed as a distinctive human accomplishment. Skeptics would deny us any such accomplishment, and the account of knowledge here is framed by confrontations with the two skeptics that I find most compelling. A lecture on dream skepticism begins the volume, and one on the problem of the criterion ends it. The core positive account of knowledge is presented in the second lecture and developed further in the fifth. These two lectures detail how the account solves the problem of external world skepticism, and the sixth how it solves the problem of the criterion. In the middle lectures the account is used to illuminate two central issues of epistemology: intuitions and their place in philosophy, in the third; and the nature of epistemic normativity, in the fourth. My overall aim is to present a kind of virtue epistemology in line with a tradition found in Aristotle, Aquinas, Reid, and especially Descartes (though none of these advocates it in all its parts), and to shine its light on varieties of skepticism, on the nature and status of intuitions, and on epistemic normativity.

At Oxford many people went out of their way to provide intellectual light and social warmth: Tim Williamson and Lizzie Fricker most of all, as well as John Broome, Jonathan

Dancy, Dorothy Edgington, John Hawthorne, Susan Hurley, Frances Kamm, Adrian Moore, Richard Price, and Chris Shields. Jeremy Butterfield and Richard Price were genial hosts at All Souls College, which provided lodgings, an office, fine wining and dining, and its enveloping charm.

I am grateful to the Oxford Philosophy Faculty for electing me to the lectureship, and extending its hospitality through its administrator, Tom Moore. Many thanks also to Peter Momtchiloff, philosophy editor at Oxford University Press, for his hospitality in Oxford, and for his good offices over the years and in connection with this two-volume work more specifically. My thanks also to Ben Fiedor and Josh Orozco for preparing the index.

I have drawn, with permission in each case, on previously published material, as detailed below, when it seemed most desirable in order to fill in the picture that I now wanted to paint on a single canvas. But the core accounts of both animal and reflective knowledge are laid out more fully than in the past, with much sharper outlines, and with a better view of their explanatory power. Lecture 1 is drawn from my Presidential Address to the Eastern Division of the American Philosophical Association, which appears in the Proceedings and Addresses of the APA, in November of 2005. Lecture 3 shares content with my "Intuitions and Truth," delivered at a St Andrews conference on truth and realism, and published in its proceedings, *Truth and Realism*, edited by Patrick Greenough and Michael Lynch (Oxford University Press, 2006). Finally, Lecture 6 is drawn from my "Two False Dichotomies: Foundationalism/Coherentism and Internalism/Externalism," delivered at a Dartmouth conference in honor of Robert Fogelin, and published in its proceedings, *Pyrrhonian Skepticism*, edited by Walter Sinnott-Armstrong (Oxford University Press, 2004).

I dedicate the book to David Sosa, dear son and prized colleague.

Lecture 1

Dreams and Philosophy

Dreams: the orthodox conception

Are dreams made up of conscious states just like those of waking life except for how they fit their surroundings? The orthodox answer is rendered poetically in Shakespeare's *The Tempest*:

> We are such stuff
> As dreams are made on and our little life
> Is rounded with a sleep . . .[1]

Dream states and waking states are thought intrinsically alike, though different in their causes and effects.

That conception is orthodox in today's common sense and also historically. Presupposed by Plato, Augustine, and Descartes, it underlies familiar skeptical paradoxes. Similar orthodoxy is also found in our developing science of sleep and dreaming.[2] Despite such confluence from common sense, philosophical tradition, and contemporary sleep science, the

---

[1] *The Tempest* IV. i. 156–7.

[2] In his *Dreaming: An Introduction to the Science of Sleep* (Oxford and New York: Oxford University Press, 2002), p. 108, Allan Hobson writes: "[Positron emission tomography studies] . . . show an *increase* in activation of just those multimodal regions of the brain that one would expect to be activated in hallucinatory perception. . . . In other words, in REM [Rapid Eye Movement] sleep—compared with waking—hallucination is enhanced."

orthodox view is deeply flawed, or so I will argue, before suggesting a better view. To dream is to imagine, not to hallucinate.

Skepticism: hyperbolic versus realistic

Skeptics propose scenarios of radical deception: the brain in a vat, Descartes' evil demon, Hollywood's Matrix. Such radical scenarios are often dismissed as "irrelevant alternatives" to our familiar common sense. They are alternative, incompatible ways that the world might have been, but not ones that are *relevant*. Why, exactly, *do* they fail the test of relevance? According to one popular view, a possibility is relevant only if it is not *too remote*, only if it might really happen. Possibilities like that of the evil demon or the brain in a vat are said to pose no real threat, being so remote.

The notion of safety thus employed is in a family that includes those of danger and of risk. These being matters of degree, we try to minimize our exposure. We keep our distance from threatening possibilities.

Skeptical scenarios are fortunately quite remote; they *might* happen, but not easily. That is why they are dismissed as irrelevant. Of all familiar scenarios, only one cannot be dismissed so easily: the most famous of all, the dream scenario. Unlike those outlandish possibilities, dreaming is a daily part of our lives.

The dream argument stands out because the dream possibility is too close for comfort. If while dreaming we have real beliefs based on real phenomenal experiences, then a normal perceptual judgment could always be matched by a subjectively similar, similarly based judgment, made while one dreams. Too easily, then, we might right now be dreaming when we form perceptual beliefs. On the orthodox conception, a dreaming subject might form such a belief in his dream, and thereby in reality. No doubt it would be a false belief, based on illusory phenomenal experience. Any given perceptual belief, or one intrinsically just like it, might thus too easily have been false though formed on the same experiential basis. This possibility, too close for comfort, threatens perceptual belief more than any radical scenario.

Fortunately, the orthodox conception is not beyond question. A lot rides epistemically on just how dreams are constituted.

What are dreams made of?

Do the characters in my dreams have beliefs and intentions? They do in general, but do I myself also have them as protagonist in my dream? Unquestionably I do believe and intend things *in my dream*.[3] In my dream I am conscious, I assent to this or that, I judge or choose.[4] This all happens *in the dream*, of course, but does it thereby *really* happen, albeit while I dream? This simple question is easy enough to grasp, but surprisingly hard to answer.

When something happens *in my dream*, reality tends not to follow suit. When in my dream I am chased by a lion, this poses no threat to my skin. No physical proposition about the

---

[3] Here I distinguish between first-person participation in the dream and third-person participation, as when one sees oneself do something as if in a movie or on a TV screen. One can figure in one's dream as a victim of a recent knockout, and would not thereby undergo any present experience.

[4] Let's here use "affirmation" for conscious assent to a propositional content and "volition" for conscious assent to a possible course of action (including simple actions, even, as a limiting case, those that are basic and instantaneous).

layout of the world around me is true in actuality just because it is true in my dream. What about mental propositions about how it is in my own mind? Must any such proposition be true in actuality whenever it is true in my dream? No, even if *in my dream* I believe that a lion is after me, and even if *in my dream* I intend to keep running, *in actuality* I have no such belief or intention. What is in question is the *inference* from <In my dream I believe (or intend) such and such> to <In actuality I so believe (or intend)>.

My exposition relies heavily on distinguishing between two expressions: "in my dream" and "while I dream." From the fact that *in my dream* something happens it does not follow that it happens *while I dream*. From the fact that in my dream I am chased by a lion it does not follow that while I dream I am chased. Moreover, from the fact that while I dream something happens, it does not follow that it happens in my dream. From the fact that while I dream it rains and thunders, it does not follow that in my dream it rains and thunders.

At any given time nearly all one's beliefs remain latent. A belief might be manifest when formed, or it might occasionally rise to consciousness from storage. To make one's belief explicit is to *judge* or *assent* or *avow*, at least to oneself.[5] The same is true of one's intentions, few of which surface at any given time. One does of course retain countless beliefs and intentions while asleep and dreaming. Among these are intentions recently formed: to stop by the library the next day, for example; and beliefs recently acquired: that the weather will be fine in the morning, say. If so, then what one knows as

---

[5] However, as will emerge, one might judge or assent or avow something that one does not believe, and even something that one disbelieves.

one dreams is that one is in bed; one lay down in the knowledge that one would be there for hours, and this knowledge has not been lost. *Lying in bed until the morning* is what one intended through most of the day, even as one thought about other things, as one had dinner, and so on. That was still one's intention as one lay down, and there is no reason to suppose that it was lost as one fell asleep. One does not lose one's intentions for the coming morning. One retains intentions as to what one *will* do upon awakening. One retains, as one drifts off to sleep, beliefs about the layout of the room: the location of one's shoes, for example, of the alarm clock, and so on. It is hard to see how one could then concurrently believe that one is being chased by a lion, rather than lying in bed, with the shoes a certain distance and direction from where one lies.[6]

Granted this for states of belief and intention, with their crucial functional profiles, perhaps conscious episodes are different. These one may perhaps *really* undergo while dreaming whenever one does so *in one's dream*. Conscious assent to a proposition does not guarantee that it is really believed, nor does conscious assent to a course of action guarantee the corresponding intention. One might even consciously assent to the opposite of what one really believes, or intends. Actions speak louder than words; louder than conscious assents, too. A deep-seated prejudice might be disavowed sincerely while still surviving, firmly entrenched. Similarly, a belief might survive in storage while consciously disavowed in a dream. Conscious affirmations and volitions might thus contradict stored beliefs and intentions, and dreams may provide just

---

[6] Might not contradictory beliefs exist in separate compartments of the mind? Perhaps. But how plausible can it be that the whole person might believe that p and *concurrently* believe also the very negation of that first belief, i.e., that not-p? This seems absurd.

a special case of that general phenomenon. The fact that one retains stored beliefs and intentions while dreaming thus seems compatible with real affirmations and volitions to the contrary, made not only in one's dream but thereby also in reality, while dreaming.

What then of propositions about your own *current* conscious states, whether conscious experiences or conscious assents? Even if you do not while dreaming really *believe* that a lion chases you, perhaps you do still consciously *affirm* it. If in a dream one is in a certain conscious state, is one then *actually* in that state, while dreaming? If in my dream I make a conscious choice, do I thereby really make that choice, while dreaming?

In a dream you may covet thy neighbor's wife, in the dream a sultry object of desire. Do you then violate the biblical injunction? If you go so far as to succumb, are you then subject to blame? Having sinned in your heart, not only in your dream, but in actuality, you could hardly escape discredit. Is one then blameworthy for choices made in a dream? That has near-zero plausibility, about as little as does blaming a storyteller for his misdeeds as protagonist in a story spun for a child. (One might blame him for telling such a story to such an audience, but that is different; one does not thereby blame him for doing what he does *in the story*.)[7]

---

[7] Compare Augustine in Book Ten, Chapter XXX of his *Confessions:* "Verily Thou enjoinest me continency from the lust of the flesh, the lust of the eyes, and the ambition of the world. Thou enjoinest continency from concubinage; and for wedlock itself, Thou hast counselled something better than what Thou hast permitted. And since Thou gavest it, it was done, even before I became a dispenser of Thy Sacrament. But there yet live in my memory (whereof I have much spoken) the images of such things as my ill custom there fixed; which haunt me, strengthless when I am awake: but in sleep, not only so as to give pleasure, but even to obtain assent, and what is very like reality. Yea, so far prevails the illusion of the image, in my soul and in my flesh, that, when asleep, false visions persuade to that which when waking, the true cannot. Am I not then myself, O Lord

If while dreaming one does *actually* assent to misdeeds, even to crimes, does its being just a dream protect one from discredit? That seems implausible. If sudden paralysis prevents you from carrying out some deplorable intentions, this does not protect you from discredit, from the full weight of the biblical injunction. How then can you be protected by the disengagement of your brain from the physical causal order? How then can you be protected by the disengagement of your inner mental life, as in a dream?

Is dreaming perhaps like being drunk or drugged? These disabling conditions lighten responsibility. Perhaps when dreaming you do make conscious choices, while your disabling state lightens your responsibility. Is *that* why we don't blame people for sins in their dreams? No, it is not that one is *less* responsible for what happens in one's dream. Rather, one is not responsible in the slightest.

Dreams seem more like imaginings, or stories, or even daydreams, all fictions of a sort, or quasi-fictions. Even when in a dream one makes a conscious choice, one need not do so in actuality. Nor does one necessarily affirm in reality whatever one consciously affirms in a dream.

What then of current *phenomenal* experiences? Does their presence in a dream entail their real presence in the conscious life of the dreamer, albeit while he dreams? Here at least,

my God? And yet there is so much difference betwixt myself and myself, within that moment wherein I pass from waking to sleeping, or return from sleeping to waking! Where is reason then, which, awake, resisteth such suggestions? And should the things themselves be urged on it, it remaineth unshaken. Is it clasped up with the eyes? Is it lulled asleep with the senses of the body? And whence is it that often even in sleep we resist, and mindful of our purpose, and abiding most chastely in it, yield no assent to such enticements? And yet so much difference there is, that when it happeneth otherwise, upon waking we return to peace of conscience: and by this very difference discover that we did not, what yet we be sorry that in some way it was done in us." (E. B. Pusey translation) it may be thought, we can plausibly draw the line. But consider the consequences. In respect of such experiences it is supposedly just as if a lion is after me. Yet I may form neither the belief that this is so nor the intention to escape. Am I not now deserving of discredit? Even if such a belief and such an intention are formed *in the dream*, they are not thereby formed *in actuality*, despite the actual experiences that would seem to require them in anyone rational. If the phenomenal experiences in dreams *are* real experiences, while dream beliefs are not real beliefs, then every night we are guilty of massive irrationality or epistemic vice.

Or so it seems at first thought. When we watch a movie, however, we undergo phenomenal experiences without being at fault for failing to take them at face value. We use them rather in an exercise of "make believe," in which our imagination is guided by what we see on the screen and hear from the sound system. We do have real visual and auditory experiences (as when we view a documentary, or the nightly news), but we have switched off our full cognitive processing for the duration of the film, so as to immerse ourselves willingly in the offline illusion. And there is no irrationality in this. Similarly, then, it may be that in vivid dreams we do have phenomenal experiences, just as we do at the movie theater, but that our full cognitive processing is switched off, enabling our immersion in the imaginative illusion of the dream.

We need not here choose between these two options on phenomenal experience. What is important for epistemology, as will emerge, is that in dreaming we do not really believe; we only make-believe.[8]

---

[8] My view on dreams is thus virtually the opposite of Colin McGinn's in his recent *Mindsight* (Cambridge, MA: Harvard University Press, 2004), where it is

Dreams and skepticism

Let us now explore what follows for philosophy from the view of dreaming as imagining.[9] If that is the right model, then traditional formulations of radical skepticism, Descartes' included, are not radical enough. The possibility that we dream now threatens not only our supposed perceptual knowledge but even our supposed introspective knowledge, our supposed takings of the given. It is now in doubt not only whether we see a fire, but even whether we *think* we see a fire, or *experience* as if we see it. How so?

With my hand in view, I may ask: do I now *think* I see a hand? Well, might it not be just a dream? Might I not be only *dreaming* that I think I see a hand? If I am only dreaming, then I do not *really* think I see a hand, after all.

If I do *ask* whether I think I see a hand, however, I cannot thereby be dreaming that I think I see a hand. If in my dream I ask myself a question, and answer it with a choice or an affirmation, the asking would seem to belong with the choice or the affirmation. If the latter belongs only in the dream, not in reality, the asking would also have its place in that same dream. So, again, if I really ask whether I think I see a hand, I cannot thereby be only dreaming that I think I see a hand. Is this not privileged access after all, protection from the possibility that it be just a dream?

argued that in dreaming we have real beliefs but not real percepts (as opposed to certain objects of imagination, called "images"). By contrast, I think that in dreaming we have no real beliefs but may well have real percepts (as we do in watching a movie or a play).

[9] The epistemological problem of dreams appears already in several passages of the *Theaetetus*, as when Socrates asks: "How can you determine whether at this moment we are sleeping, and all our thoughts are a dream; or whether we are awake, and talking to one another in the waking state?"

Fair enough. But compare my question whether I *see* a hand. If I really *ask* whether I see a hand, I cannot thereby be dreaming about the hand and my seeing it. So, we seem to have similarly privileged access to the fact that we see a hand, at least similarly privileged *in respect of protection from the dream argument*.

What might possibly make the *cogito especially* privileged? What could give it a status not shared by perception of the hand? One advantage at least it turns out *not* to enjoy: it enjoys no special protection from the possibility that one is only dreaming.

The *cogito* has got to be different nonetheless from our knowledge of a hand we see. We might try to defend the *cogito* by retreating to a thinner, less committing, concept of thinking, where even dreaming and imagining are themselves forms of "thinking." On the *thicker* notion of thinking, if I imagine that p, hypothesize that p, or dream that p, I do not *thereby* think that p; I may not even think that p at all. On the *thinner* notion of thinking, by contrast, in imagining that p one *does* thereby think that p. And the same is now true of dreaming. On the thinner notion, in dreaming that p, one does thereby think that p. More idiomatically, let's say rather this: in dreaming or imagining that p, one *has the thought that p*. So, "thinking that p" in the thinner sense would amount to "having the thought that p," a thought one can have even by just asking oneself whether p.

Compare (a) one's affirming that one affirms something, with (b) one's having (the thought) that one has a thought. The latter is also a self-verifying (thin) thought. But it has in addition something missing from the former: namely, being dream-proof. If one were now dreaming, one would affirm nothing. But one would still have the thought that one was having a thought.

So, my present thought that I am having a thought is not only guaranteed to be right; in addition, I would not so much as *seem* to have it without having it, not even if I were dreaming. Compare my *affirming* that I am affirming something. This too is guaranteed to be right. But, unlike the thinner thought, it *could* be mere appearance. I might right now be dreaming that I was affirming something, while in fact affirming nothing. So, things might in a way seem subjectively just as they do now, although I would *just* be dreaming: thoughts would be crossing my mind, without my really affirming anything.

However, the more defensible thinner thought falls short crucially in the dialectic against the skeptic. It is not the sort of thought that suffices to constitute knowledge. Knowledge requires something thicker than merely having a thought. Accordingly, the move from thick thought to thin thought is not a way to save the *cogito*, after all.

Consciously and affirmatively thinking that I think does have a special status: one could not go wrong in so thinking. It can thus attain high reliability and epistemic status. It attains this status through its *being* a conscious state of thinking that one thinks. Moreover, this status is not removed, or even much diminished, by the threat of an impostor state, one subjectively very much like it. A vivid and realistic dream is, of course, subjectively very much like its corresponding reality.[10] Perhaps it is only *in my dream* that I now affirmatively think that I think. Despite being subjectively much like the state of thinking that one thinks, in dreaming one does *not*

---

[10] Much as someone with a powerful visual imagination can picture a scene so vividly that the imagined scene and the one earlier seen are very much alike in content, despite the failure of the two conscious states to share any actual sensory experiences.

think; one does not so much as think that one thinks. That is to say, even if *in one's dream* one affirmatively thinks that one thinks, this does not entail that in reality one so thinks that one thinks, while dreaming.

Two states can thus be hard to distinguish subjectively, though in only one is the subject justified in thinking such and such. Of course the two states are constitutively different. One is an apparent state of thinking one thinks, doing so (thinking one thinks) *only in a dream*, so that it is really only a state of *dreaming* that one thinks one thinks. By contrast, the other is a state of thinking one thinks, doing so (thinking one thinks) *in actuality*. Only the latter yields justification for one's thought that one thinks. The former not only yields no such justification: in it there *is* no such thought—this despite the fact that, by hypothesis, the two states are indistinguishable, as indistinguishable as is reality from a realistic enough dream.[11]

Have we here found a way to defend our perceptual knowledge from the skeptic's dream argument? Even if we might just as easily be dreaming that we see a hand, this does not entail that we might now be astray in our perceptual beliefs. For, even if we might be dreaming, it does not follow that we might be thinking we see a hand on this same experiential basis, without seeing any hand. After all, in dreaming there is no real thinking and perhaps not even any real experiencing. So, even if I had now been dreaming,

---

[11] This is not to say that there are no important intrinsic and relational differences between a realistic dream and a correlative stretch of waking life. It is only to say that in a very realistic dream we take the goings-on to be certainly real, which leads naturally to the thought that "this," referring to the contents of one's present waking consciousness, insofar as one takes notice of them, could all be (the contents of) a dream. One could of course protest that though *in the dream* one is taken in, this does not show that one's *waking* consciousness could mislead in that way. The topic is far from exhausted, however; we return to it below.

which might easily enough have happened, I would not thereby have been thinking that I see a hand, based on a corresponding phenomenal experience.[12]

That disposes of the threat posed by dreams for the safety of our beliefs. Does it dispose of the problem of dream skepticism? It does so if dreams create such a problem only by threatening the safety of our perceptual beliefs. *Is* that the only threat posed by dreams? We next take up this question.

Are dreams indistinguishable in a way that matters?

One need not be a Freudian to believe that dreams have causes, in which case most of us might be picked at random, in a futuristic scenario, and made to dream in a connected, realistic way so that our lives become lengthy dreams. Under that Matrix-like supposition, can I be said to know that I now see a hand? I might of course be dreaming in a maximally realistic way that I see a hand. Could I reason my way out by noting that, since I am wondering whether this is just a dream, *therefore* I cannot be dreaming? Can I conclude that this must be reality, not a dream, and that I really do see a hand? No, that certainly would not satisfy. If I wonder

[12] I argue in "Skepticism and the Internal/External Divide" (in J. Greco and E. Sosa (eds.), *The Blackwell Guide to Epistemology* (Cambridge, MA, and Oxford, UK: Blackwell, 1999), pp. 145–58) that rational intuition has a similar epistemic profile: that one could be intuitively justified in believing that p even though in another situation, not distinguishable in any relevant subjectively accessible respect, one still would not be intuitively justified in believing that q. Though subtly different from our conclusion about the *cogito* and dreams, it is closely related. In both cases, it seems that one can be in relevantly indistinguishable situations, yet epistemically justified in only one of them.

whether I am one of the dreamers in the first place, my doubt must extend to whether I am *really* wondering, or only *dreaming* that I am wondering.

Knowledge seems to require more than just safety. As we have seen, on the imagination model, the *safety* of one's belief is not affected by the nearby possibility of a realistic dream. Still, the skeptical force of the internally indistinguishable dream seems undeniable even so. The dream possibility still threatens, even if it is no threat to the *safety* of our beliefs.

How then *are* dreams a threat? What they threaten is not the safety of our beliefs but perhaps their rationality. Can it be rationally coherent to grant that one could be dreaming? How can one rationally allow that possibility, as one must do if unable to rule it out? That would seem incoherent, but exactly how?

Let us step back. Suppose I could now about as easily be dead, having barely escaped a potentially fatal accident. Obviously, I cannot distinguish my being alive from being dead by believing myself alive when alive, and dead when dead. Similarly, I cannot distinguish my being conscious from my being unconscious by attributing to myself consciousness when conscious and unconsciousness when unconscious. But that is no obstacle to my knowing myself alive and conscious when alive and conscious. Might the possibility that we dream not be like that of being dead, or unconscious? Even if one could never tell *that* one suffers such a fate, one can still tell that one does *not* suffer it when one does not.[13] Why not say the same of dreams?

---

[13] Cf. B. Williams, *Descartes: The Project of Pure Inquiry* (London: Penguin Books, 1978), Appendix 3.

Even if we are unable to specify how a Matrix dream scenario is epistemically different from the possibility that one is dead or unconscious, this does little to reassure us. How can I know that I see a hand, once I posit that I could be just dreaming in a Matrix scenario, when only by astronomical luck could I be among the spared? *Something* seems to distinguish the possibility that one now dreams in such a scenario from the possibility that one be dead or unconscious, even if we cannot specify what the difference is, exactly.[14] We still face a threat of irrationality.

Note the first-person way in which the problem is posed. Evaluation of someone else is importantly different; to someone else we might more plausibly attribute knowledge even if they could as easily be dreaming. It pays to distinguish here between animal knowledge and reflective knowledge. When I ask myself whether I know I see a hand even if I might just be dreaming, I take a reflective perspective on my own knowledge. Suppose that, so far as I know, *this (referring to the contents of my present states of consciousness) could all about as easily be the contents of a dream.* In that case, it would seem less coherent for me to believe that I am awake nonetheless.

What more specifically constitutes the threat to our rationality? Is it the arbitrariness in taking myself to be awake? When awake we automatically take ourselves to be awake, rather than dreaming an internally indistinguishable dream. Can that be rational, when nothing in the content of our conscious states would seem to reveal that difference? True,

---

[14] And the same may apply to the possibility that one is mentally disabled, though in important respects this belongs in a category with dreams, both being eventualities that, too easily for full epistemic comfort, might right now be happening; it will depend on how the possibility of one's being disabled is filled out.

waking states *are* different *in kind* from dream states. In waking life I would *see* a hand, for example, which is different from only *dreaming* that I do. Nevertheless, if while awake I see or believe certain things, *in the corresponding dream* I would also see and believe the very same things, provided my dream was vivid and realistic enough. How then can I non-arbitrarily take myself to be awake, when I cannot distinguish my state internally from that of a realistic dream? Of course that does not prevent my taking it for granted that I am awake. But how can this be more than just arbitrary?

At an unreflective level, epistemic justification can hence derive from the holding of a condition whose absence is no more subjectively distinguishable from its presence than is a realistic dream from waking life. Still, without reflective, non-arbitrary assurance that you satisfy that condition, you cannot know reflectively something you might still know at the animal level. So far at least, we have found no way out of this predicament. Reflectively defensible perceptual knowledge still seems out of reach.

How to resolve the problem of dream skepticism

In conclusion, here is a way out. Consider the claim that one is just dreaming, which could not possibly be affirmed correctly, and is hence pragmatically incoherent. Or take the contradictory claim: that one is *not* just dreaming, which, like the *cogito*, must be right if affirmed. We can now see, reflectively, how these thoughts gain their special status. The impossibility of being affirmed falsely is thought to help give the *cogito* a special status, which we can reflectively see that it has. The claim that one is not now just dreaming, being equally impossible to affirm falsely, must have an equally high epistemic status, equally defensible reflectively. For it seems to share with the *cogito* its pragmatic safety, and its epistemically favorable features more generally, such as a high degree of self-intimation: when one is awake and one asks oneself whether one is awake, one has a very strong tendency to answer affirmatively.

One can distinguish being alive from being dead when indeed one is. It does not matter that one *cannot* tell that one is dead rather than alive, when *that* is how it is. One can also distinguish being conscious from being unconscious if one can tell that one is conscious rather than unconscious when indeed one is. It does not matter that one *cannot* tell that one is unconscious rather than conscious, when *that* is how it is.[15]

That suggests a way out of our paradox, even if it has us *distinguish* waking life from a corresponding dream despite the lack of any discernible difference of content. What enables us to distinguish the two content-identical states is just the fact that in the dream state we do not affirm *anything*—not that we are veridically perceiving an external world, nor that we are not—whereas in waking life we do knowingly perceive

---

[15] Bernard Williams's response to dream skepticism is like mine in one important respect (op. cit., n.14 of Lecture I), but is substantially different and incompatible on the whole. We both rely on what dreaming shares with being unconscious or dead: i.e., we both rely on your ability to tell that you avoid such a fate, when you do, despite your inability to tell that the fate befalls you when it does. The crucial respect of difference is that for Williams we do have real conscious beliefs and experiences in dreaming. Unlike my account, his preserves the special protection of the *cogito* against dream skepticism, for even if one is dreaming, when one thinks that one thinks (really thinks) one does really think, really believe consciously, or really experience, etc. Correlatively, he is also denied access to my proposed solution for the problem of dream skepticism, whether the solution is applied to the *cogito* or to the fire; according to my proposal, <I am hereby awake> shares the special epistemic status of the *cogito*.

our surroundings. *This* by our lights suffices to make the two states distinguishable.[16]

Suppose I have only three possible options on the question whether p, which I am now pondering: namely, the options of believing, suspending, or disbelieving, all consciously, since I am consciously pondering my question now. If I know that only one of my options is epistemically undefective, making it the best option, that then would seem the rational option for me to take.

Consider a *cogito* proposition, such as <I think> or <I am>. Disbelieving is in these cases defective, since self-defeating, for I know that if I take that option I will be wrong.[17] Suspending is also defective, but in a different way.

---

[16] We must accordingly reconsider whether waking life is really indistinguishable from a realistic enough dream. Here is how we had implicitly understood what it is to be indistinguishable:

> A possible extended dream and a possible stream of waking consciousness are *indistinguishable* if, and only if, no possible conscious content is at any time contained in either without being contained in both.

Of course, under this definition it is trivial that waking life is indistinguishable from a realistic corresponding dream. But that is not the only plausible way to understand what it is to be indistinguishable. Here is another way:

> Two scenarios are *indistinguishable* if, and only if, one can tell *neither* that one is in the first and not the second when that is so, *nor* that one is in the second and not the first when *that* is so.

One can thus distinguish being conscious from being unconscious if one can tell that one is conscious rather than unconscious when indeed one is. It does not matter that one *cannot* tell that one is unconscious rather than conscious, when *that* is how it is. (Alternatively, one might define what it is for state X to be distinguishable from state Y, and then point out that this relation is not symmetric.)

[17] "[I]f I am deceived, I am. For he who does not exist cannot be deceived; and if I am deceived, by this same token I am." St Augustine, *The Essential Augustine*, 2nd edn, selected and with commentary by Vernon J. Bourke (Indianapolis, IN:

For, I know, about a particular alternative option, that I am epistemically better off if I take that other option, since I will thereby avail myself of a correct answer to my question, which I fail to do if I only suspend judgment. Only the believing option is not defective in this sort of way. Only that option is such that I will *not* then be epistemically better off taking either one of the other available options. On the contrary, as I ponder the question whether I think and exist, as I epistemically deliberate, the believing option is the only one about which I know ahead of time that my taking it will obviously imply that I am epistemically right in so doing.

On the imagination model of dreaming <I am awake> shares the noted epistemic status of *cogito* propositions. In its case too, believing is the only epistemically undefective option. Both suspending judgment and disbelieving will share the following feature: that I know ahead of time, as I ponder my question, that I am better off epistemically if I take a particular other option, namely the belief option, since only about that option is it obvious to me now that if I take it I will be right.[18]

Hackett Publishing Company, 1973). "If I am Deceived, I Exist," at 33; source of the translation: *City of God*, XI. 26; trans. *The Works of Aurelius Augustinus*, ed. Marcus Dods, 15 vols (Edinburgh: T. & T. Clark Co., 1871–6), revised by Vernon J. Bourke.

[18] In my view there are at least two ways to fail to be awake. One might be entirely unconscious, whether by sleeping deeply enough or by having lost consciousness in some other way, perhaps as victim of a knockout. Alternatively, one might be conscious while one's state of consciousness is entirely filled by dreaming. It is of course compatible with this (partial) account that in lucid dreaming one is dreaming awake. Lucid dreaming thus becomes a kind of daydreaming, which can come in different varieties, depending, for example, on how much control one enjoys over the proceedings. Suppose you lucidly dream that you face a fire. On the imagination model we are still protected from the dream skeptic. For you will believe that you face a fire *only in the dream*. And from this it does not follow that you really believe it, while you dream. Nor,

What alternative is there to our proposed approach? Should one think that for all we know our current conscious life is nothing but a dream? Given our conception of dreams, how could one even sensibly entertain that possibility? If one *is* only dreaming, then one cannot be pondering any such question as whether one might be only dreaming, and one could not possibly assent to any answer, whether affirmative or negative. Knowing this, how can one sensibly deliberate on whether one might be dreaming? On our conception of dreams, one is automatically, rationally *committed* to supposing that one is *not* just dreaming, whenever one inquires at all. It is hard to imagine a better answer to the dream skeptic. On this view, knowledge of a fire that I see is no less defensible from dream skepticism than is knowledge of the *cogito*. We can just as well affirm <I think, therefore I am awake> as <I think, therefore I am>.[19]

presumably, would the lucid dreamer, who believes the dream to be a dream, be misled into thinking he faces a real fire just because in his dream he does so. In any case, on the present account, <I am awake> remains self-confirming in the way of the *cogito*, as does of course <I am *hereby* awake>.

[19] My interest in dreams and skepticism goes back a long time, and the imagination model has figured in my preferred approach for many years, in courses and seminars. In the spring and summer of 2003 I presented these ideas in more formal settings, at a University of Florida conference in April, and at the Wittgenstein Symposium that summer (later published in its proceedings, *Knowledge and Belief. Wissen und Glaben* (ÖBV&HPT Publishers, 2005), ed. Winfried Löffler and Paul Weingartner, pp. 228–36). I remember helpful comments by Dan Kaufman, Jaegwon Kim, and Kirk Ludwig at the Florida conference, and good discussion with Robert Audi and Jay Rosenberg at the Kirchberg conference.

More recently I have become aware that in his *Mindsight* (Harvard, 2004), Colin McGinn develops similar ideas about the nature of dreams (which he traces back to Jean-Paul Sartre's *The Psychology of Imagination*). Although each account was developed in total ignorance of the other, there is a lot of agreement between us. But there are also important differences and even substantial disagreement. Much of my interest in these issues involves philosophical skepticism, for example, and here we have a looming disagreement. For him, we form beliefs not only in our dreams but also thereby while we dream. At this epistemologically crucial

Having ostensibly rescued our reflective knowledge from the dream skeptic, we still face a further threat, from the more radical skeptical scenarios. How can we non-arbitrarily take ourselves to be safe from these? Unless we can do so, we still fall short of reflective knowledge. We take this up in the second and fifth lectures.

juncture we part ways, as we do also on basic ontological and epistemological issues concerning dreams and the imagination.

Lecture 2

A Virtue Epistemology

When an archer takes aim and shoots, that shot is assessable in three respects.

First, we can assess whether it succeeds in its aim, in hitting the target. Although we can also assess how accurate a shot it is, how close to the bull's-eye, we here put degrees aside, in favor of the on/off question: whether it hits the target or not.

Second, we can assess whether it is adroit, whether it manifests skill on the part of the archer. Skill too comes in degrees, but here again we focus on the on/off question: whether it manifests relevant skill or not, whether it is or is not adroit.

A shot can be both accurate and adroit, however, without being a success creditable to its author. Take a shot that in normal conditions would have hit the bull's-eye. The wind may be abnormally strong, and just strong enough to divert the arrow so that, in conditions thereafter normal, it would miss the target altogether. However, shifting winds may next guide it gently to the bull's-eye after all. The shot is then accurate and adroit, but not accurate *because* adroit (not sufficiently). So it is not apt, and not creditable to the archer.[1]

An archer's shot is thus a performance that can have the AAA structure: accuracy, adroitness, aptness. So can

---

[1] Aptness is a matter of degree even beyond the degrees imported by its constitutive adroitness and accuracy, for a performance is apt only if its success is *sufficiently* attributable to the performer's competence.

performances generally, at least those that have an aim, even if the aim is not intentional. A shot succeeds if it is aimed intentionally to hit a target and does so. A heartbeat succeeds if it helps pump blood, even absent any intentional aim.

Maybe all performances have an aim, even those super-ficially aimless, such as ostensibly aimless ambling. Perform-ances with an aim, in any case, admit assessment in respect of our three attainments: accuracy: reaching the aim; adroitness: manifesting skill or competence; and aptness: reaching the aim *through* the adroitness manifest. The following will be restricted to performances with an aim.

Some acts are performances, of course, but so are some sustained states. Think of those live motionless statues that one sees at tourist sites. Such performances can linger, and need not be constantly sustained through renewed conscious intentions. The performer's mind could wander, with little effect on the continuation or quality of the performance.

Beliefs too might thus count as performances, long-sustained ones, with no more conscious or intentional an aim than that of a heartbeat. At a minimum, beliefs can be assessed for correctness independently of any competence that they may manifest. Beliefs can be true by luck, after all, independently of the believer's competence in so believing, as in Gettier cases.

Beliefs fall under the AAA structure, as do performances generally. We can distinguish between a belief's accuracy, i.e., its truth; its adroitness, i.e., its manifesting epistemic virtue or competence; and its aptness, i.e., its being true *because* competent.[2]

---

[2] Compare: "We have reached the view that knowledge is true belief out of intellectual virtue, belief that turns out right by reason of the virtue and not just by

Animal knowledge is essentially apt belief, as distinguished from the more demanding reflective knowledge. This is not to say that the word "knows" is ambiguous. Maybe it is, but distinguishing a kind of knowledge as "animal" knowledge requires no commitment to that linguistic thesis. Indeed, despite leaving the word "knows" undefined, one might proceed in three stages as follows:

(a) affirm that knowledge entails belief;
(b) understand "animal" knowledge as requiring apt belief *without* requiring *defensibly* apt belief, i.e., apt belief that the subject aptly believes to be apt, and whose aptness the subject can therefore defend against relevant skeptical doubts; and
(c) understand "reflective" knowledge as requiring not only apt belief but *also* defensibly apt belief.

There you have the core ideas of the virtue epistemology to be developed in the remaining lectures.

coincidence." (Sosa, *Knowledge in Perspective* (Cambridge: Cambridge University Press, 1991), p. 277). Also: "What in sum is required for knowledge and what are the roles of intellectual virtue and perspective? . . . [One] must grasp that one's belief non-accidentally reflects the truth [of the proposition known] through the exercise of such a virtue" (Sosa, 1991, p. 292). Also: "We need a clearer and more comprehensive view of the respects in which one's belief must *be non-accidentally true* if it is to constitute knowledge. Unaided, the tracking or causal requirements proposed . . . permit too narrow a focus on the particular target belief and its causal or counterfactual relation to the *truth* of its content. Just widening our focus will not do, however, if we widen it only far enough to include the process that yields the belief involved. We need an even broader view" (Sosa, "Reflective Knowledge in the Best Circles," *The Journal of Philosophy* (1997): 410–30), from the sections entitled "Circular Externalism" and "Virtue Epistemology"; emphasis added). That broader view, as explained soon thereafter, puts the emphasis on the subject and on the subject's virtues or competences. And it is made clear that the belief must be non-accidentally true, and not just non-accidentally present. The view developed in the present paper is essentially that same view, now better formulated, based on an improved conception of aptness, and explicitly amplified to cover performances generally.

One other idea has also been part of virtue epistemology, that of the *safety* of a belief. This too is a special case of an idea applicable to performances generally. A performance is safe if and only if not easily would it then have failed, not easily would it have fallen short of its aim. What is required for the safety of a belief is that not easily would it fail by being false, or untrue. A belief that p is *safe* provided it would have been held only if (most likely) p.

By contrast, someone's belief that p is *sensitive* if and only if were it not so that p, he would not (likely) believe that p.

Surprisingly enough, such conditionals do not contrapose. Suppose that if it were so that p, then it would be so that q. It might seem to follow that if it were *not* so that q, then it would *not* be so that p. After all, if it were *not* so that q while it was still so that p, it *would* then be so that p *without* it being so that q. How then could it be that if it were so that p, it would be so that q? It is thus quite plausible to think that such conditionals contrapose, as do material conditionals; plausible, but still incorrect. If water now flowed from your kitchen faucet, for example, it would then be false that water so flowed while your main house valve was closed. But the contrapositive of this true conditional is false.

Accordingly, a belief can be safe without being sensitive. Radical skeptical scenarios provide examples. Take one's belief that one is not a brain in a vat fooled by misleading sensory evidence into so believing. That belief is safe without being sensitive. We can thus defend Moorean common sense by highlighting the skeptic's confusion of safety with sensitivity. Although our belief that we are not radically fooled is not sensitive, it is still safe, since not easily would that belief be false. Radical scenarios are ones that not easily would materialize.

That defense against radical skepticism is soon halted by beliefs that seem unsafe while still amounting to knowledge. I am hit hard and suffer excruciating pain, perhaps, believing on that basis that I am in pain. But I might very easily have suffered only a slight glancing blow instead, experiencing only discomfort, while still believing myself to suffer pain. This might have been due to priming, perhaps, or to hypochondria. Nevertheless, I do know I suffer pain when the pain is excruciating, surely, even if my belief is unsafe because I might too easily have so believed in the presence of discomfort that was not really pain.

What knowledge requires is hence not outright safety but at most basis–relative safety. What is required of one's belief, if it is to constitute knowledge, is at most its having some basis that it would not easily have had unless true, some basis that it would (likely) have had only if true. When your belief that you are in pain is based on your excruciating pain, it satisfies this requirement: it would not easily have been so based unless true, it would (likely) have been so based only if true. And this is so despite its *not* being safe outright, since you might too easily have believed that you were in pain while suffering only discomfort and not pain.

A belief that p is *basis-relative safe*, then, if and only if it has a basis that it would (likely) have only if true. By contrast, a belief that p is *basis-relative sensitive* if and only if it is based on a basis such that if it were false that p, then not easily would the believer believe that p on that same basis.

More plausibly, then, what is properly required for knowledge is basis–relative safety, rather than outright safety.

The radical skeptic claims, about some epistemologically crucial beliefs, that they have no basis they would lack if false. If you were deceived based on radically misleading experience, for example, you would still believe that you were *not* so deceived, and there need be no basis that you now have for that belief which you would then lack.

In so reasoning, the skeptic restricts us to bases for belief that are purely internal and psychological, by contrast with those that are external. Otherwise, his main premise would collapse. If we allow external bases, then the brain in a vat will no doubt lack some basis that sustains our ordinary belief that we are normally embodied. The skeptic's internalist assumption has of course been challenged in recent years, but here I will grant it for the sake of argument. I wish to explore a different line of defense, a virtue epistemology that is compatible with but not committed to content or basis externalism. Part of the interest of this line of defense may indeed derive from the fact that it does *not* depend on such externalism.

What then is the alternative defense? It proceeds as follows:

(a) reject the skeptic's requirement of outright sensitivity, and even his requirement of basis-relative sensitivity;

(b) point out the intuitive advantage, over such sensitivity requirements, enjoyed by corresponding safety requirements;

(c) suggest that the plausibility of the sensitivity requirements derives from the corresponding safety requirements so easily confused with them through failure to appreciate that strong conditionals do not contrapose;

(d) conclude that the skeptic does not refute common sense, nor does he even locate a paradox within common sense, since we are commonsensically committed at most to basis-relative safety, and not to basis-relative sensitivity; for, our belief that we are not radically deceived—as in a

brain-in-a-vat or evil-demon scenario—is basis-relative
safe, though not basis-relative sensitive.

Although quite plausible against radical scenarios, that
defense falls short against the one traditional scenario that
does not depend on remote possibilities, namely the dream
scenario. That scenario is most useful to the skeptic on
the orthodox conception according to which the episodes
of consciousness that we undergo in our dreams are ones
that we thereby really undergo, while we dream. I have
challenged that orthodox conception in my first lecture,
while proposing that dreaming is much more like imagining
than like hallucinating. But let us here set aside that challenge,
in order to explore an alternative solution to the problem
of dreams, one with its own distinctive interest and more
directly in line with our virtue epistemology.

I would like to confront dream skepticism directly, without
presupposing the imagination model. Indeed, let us initially
grant to the skeptic the orthodox conception required for the
dream-based attack. How might a virtue epistemology help
thwart that attack?

Return first to our archer's shot. There are at least two
interesting ways in which that shot might fail to be safe: I
mean, two ways in which that archer might then too easily
have released that arrow from that bow aimed at that target
while the shot failed. The following two things might each
have been fragile enough to deprive that shot of safety:
(a) the archer's level of competence, for one, and (b) the
appropriateness of the conditions, for another.

Thus (a) the archer might have recently ingested a drug,
so that at the moment when he aimed and shot, his blood

content of the drug might too easily have been slightly higher, so as to reduce his competence to where he would surely have missed. Or else (b) a freak set of meteorological conditions might have gathered in such a way that too easily a gust might have diverted the arrow on its way to the target.

In neither case, however, would the archer be denied credit for his fine shot simply because it is thus unsafe. The shot is apt and creditable even if its aptness is thus fragile. What is required for the shot to be apt is that it be accurate because adroit, successful because competent. That it might too easily have failed through reduced competence or degraded conditions renders it unsafe but not inapt.

So we have seen ways in which a performance can be apt though unsafe. Moreover, a performance might be safe though inapt. A protecting angel with a wind machine might ensure that the archer's shot would hit the bull's-eye, for example, and a particular shot might hit the bull's-eye through a gust from the angel's machine, which compensates for a natural gust that initially diverts the arrow. In this case the shot is safe without being apt: it is not accurate *because* adroit.

In conclusion, neither aptness nor safety entails the other. The connection that perhaps remains is only this. Aptness requires the manifestation of a competence, and a competence is a disposition, one with a basis resident in the competent agent, one that would in appropriately normal conditions ensure (or make highly likely) the success of any relevant performance issued by it. Compatibly with such restricted safety, the competence manifest might then be fragile, as might also the appropriate normalcy of the conditions in which it is manifest.

The bearing of those reflections on the problem of dreams is now straightforward. True, on the orthodox conception dreams do pose a danger for our perceptual beliefs, which are *un*safe through the nearness of the dream possibility, wherein one is said to host such a belief on the same sensory basis while dreaming. However, what dreams render vulnerable is only this: either the perceptual competence of the believer or the appropriate normalcy of the conditions for its exercise.

The dreamer's experience may be fragmentary and indistinct, so that his sensory basis may not be quite the same as that of a normal perceiver. Recall Austin's "dreamlike" quality of dreams,[3] and Descartes' idea that dreams are insufficiently coherent.[4] However, the dreamer's reduced or lost competence may blind him to such features of his experience, features that would enable him to distinguish dreaming from perceiving. Sleep might render one's conditions abnormal and inadequate for the exercise of perceptual faculties. The proximate possibility that one is now asleep and dreaming might thus render fragile both one's competence and also, jointly or alternatively, the conditions appropriate for its exercise. That is how the possibility that one is asleep and dreaming might endanger our ordinary perceptual beliefs. But this is just one more case where safety is compromised while aptness remains intact.

Ordinary perceptual beliefs might thus retain their status as apt, animal knowledge, despite the possibility that one is asleep and dreaming. Ordinary perceptual beliefs can still attain success through the exercise of perceptual competence, despite the fragility of that competence and of its required

---

[3] In *Sense and Sensibilia* (Oxford: Oxford University Press, 1962).
[4] In Meditation Six.

conditions. However unsafe a performer's competence may be, and however unsafe may be the conditions appropriate for its exercise, if a performance does succeed through the exercise of that competence in its proper conditions, then it is an apt performance, one creditable to the performer. Knowledge is just a special case of such creditable, apt performance. Perceptual knowledge is unaffected by any fragility either in the knower's competence or in the conditions appropriate for its exercise. The knower's belief can thus remain apt even if unsafe through the proximity of the dream possibility.

Despite how plausible that may seem intuitively, we soon encounter a problem. You see a surface that looks red in ostensibly normal conditions. But it is a kaleidoscope surface controlled by a jokester who also controls the ambient light, and might as easily have presented you with a red-light+white-surface combination as with the actual white-light+red-surface combination. Do you then know the surface you see to be red when he presents you with that good combination, despite the fact that, even more easily, he might have presented you with the bad combination?

Arguably, your belief that the surface is red is an apt belief, in which case it amounts to knowledge, or so it does according to our account. For you then exercise your faculty of color vision in normal conditions of lighting, distance, size of surface, etc., in conditions generally appropriate for the exercise of color vision. Yet it is not easy to insist that you therefore *know* that surface to be red.

If forced to retreat along that line, our solution to the problem of dreams will be undone. For we will not be able to insist that, despite the proximity of the dream possibility, perceptual beliefs are nonetheless apt and therefore knowledge. Apt they may still be, but no longer clearly knowledge. Of course, we could still fall back to the imagination model, but our solution directly through a virtue epistemology would have vanished.

Recall, however, our distinction between two sorts of knowledge, the animal and the reflective. Any full account would need to register how these are matters of degree. For present purposes, however, the key component of the distinction is the difference between apt belief *simpliciter*, and apt belief aptly noted. If K represents animal knowledge and K^+ reflective knowledge, then the basic idea may be represented thus: $K^+p \leftrightarrow KKp$.

That is a distinction worth deploying on the kaleidoscope example. The perceiver would there be said to have apt belief, and animal knowledge, that the seen surface is red. What he lacks, we may now add, is *reflective* knowledge, since this requires apt belief that he aptly believes the surface to be red (or at least it requires that he aptly take this for granted, or assume it or presuppose it, a qualification implicit in what follows).

Why should it be any less plausible to think that he aptly believes that he aptly believes than to think that he aptly believes *simpliciter*? Well, what competence might he exercise in believing that he aptly so believes, and how plausible might it be to attribute to that competence his being right in believing that he aptly believes?

What, for example, is the competence we exercise in taking the light to be normal when we trust our color vision in an ordinary case? It seems a kind of default competence, whereby one automatically takes the light to be normal absent some special indication to the contrary. And that is presumably what the kaleidoscope perceiver does, absent any indication of a jokester in control. So, we may suppose him to retain that competence unimpaired *and* to exercise it in taking for granted the adequacy of the ambient light, so that he can aptly take the surface to be red. Since the belief that he believes aptly is a *true* belief, and since it is *owed* to the exercise of a competence, how then can we suppose it not to be itself an apt belief? Well, recall: the requirement for aptly believing is not just that one's belief be true, and derive from a competence. The requirement is rather that one believe *correctly* (with truth) through the exercise of a competence in its proper conditions. What must be attributable to the competence is not just the belief's existence but its correctness.

Here now is a premise from which I propose to argue:

C. For any correct belief that p, the correctness of that belief is attributable to a competence only if it derives from the exercise of that competence in appropriate conditions for its exercise, and that exercise in those conditions would not then too easily have issued a false belief.

Consider now the kaleidoscope perceiver's belief that he aptly believes the seen surface to be red. We are assuming that the competence exercised in that meta-belief is a default competence, one which, absent any specific indication to the contrary, takes it for granted that, for example, the lights are normal. Because of the jokester in control, however, the exercise of that competence might then too easily have issued a false belief that the lights are normal. Given principle C, therefore, we must deny that the truth of our perceiver's belief that he aptly believes the surface to be red is *attributable to his relevant competence*. There being no other relevant competence in view, we must deny that the perceiver *aptly* believes that he aptly believes the surface to be red. Nor can the perceiver then have animal knowledge that he has animal knowledge that the surface is red. And that is why the perceiver then lacks reflective knowledge of the color of that surface.

What shall we now say of the problem of dreams? If it is analogous to the kaleidoscope problem, then, although we can defend our perceptual beliefs as apt, we must surrender to the dream skeptic their status as reflectively defensible. We can defend our perceptual beliefs as cases of animal knowledge, but must relinquish any claim to the higher status of reflective knowledge. Surrender seems hasty, though; let's retreat and reconsider.

The problem of dreams arises for any ordinary case of perceptual knowledge through the fact that the subject might too easily have believed just as he does in that instance, although his belief and its sensory basis would have been housed in a dream. Too easily, then, might any ordinary perceptual belief have had its same basis while false.

Although ordinary perceptual beliefs *are* thus rendered unsafe, we responded, they can remain apt even so, and hence knowledge of a sort, of the animal sort. What is endangered by the dream possibility is only our perceptual competence or the presence of appropriate conditions for its exercise. But this poses no danger to the aptness of beliefs yielded by perceptual competence in appropriately normal conditions, and only aptness is required for animal knowledge, not safety.

However, the kaleidoscope case puts that response in doubt. What seems there endangered is one's perceptual competence or the conditions for its exercise, yet we are strongly drawn to claim that although one's belief is apt it is not knowledge.

It helps to distinguish between animal and reflective knowledge, between apt belief *simpliciter*, and apt belief aptly noted. That distinction helps us defend the kaleidoscope perceiver's knowledge as a case of *animal* knowledge. We thus implicitly suggest that he has knowledge of a sort, animal knowledge, while lacking knowledge of another sort, reflective knowledge. So, if we apply our reasoning about that case to the problem of dreams, the consequence will be that perceptual knowledge generally falls short of the reflective level. The skeptic wins.

If common sense is to prevail, based on our virtue epistemology, we must see how, in ordinary perceptual belief, one can aptly presuppose, or take it for granted, that the relevant competence and conditions are in place. But the aptness of any such presupposition would require that it be correct because of a competence exercised in the conditions in which it is exercised. And the relevant competence seems nothing more than a default competence of assuming ourselves awake whenever conscious, absent any specific indication to the contrary. But the ease with which we might have gone wrong by so presupposing on such a basis is proportional to the proximity of the dream possibility, and that is really too close for comfort. So we would have to conclude that our getting it right when we ordinarily believe ourselves awake is not attributable (sufficiently) to the exercise of our default competence. That is the conclusion to which we are led by reasoning from principle C above. We do not get it right through competence in presupposing ourselves awake, since the supposed competence that we exercise, in its proper conditions, might too easily lead us astray.

That is where we are led if we take our cue, for ordinary perception in general, from the kaleidoscope example. In that example, we retain animal knowledge because we seem clearly enough to exercise our color vision in its normal conditions (of distance, lighting, size of surface, etc.). There we fall short of reflective knowledge, however, because the jokester precludes the aptness of our implicit confidence that our perceptual belief is apt. His being in control makes it too easy for us to be confident in that default way, in normal conditions for the exercise of our perceptual competence, while still mistaken. So when, as it happens, we are right, not mistaken, this cannot be attributed to the exercise of our default competence as a success derived from it.

It might well be thought that the presence of the jokester makes our conditions abnormal for presupposing that the light is good. But in so presupposing we must then fall short of aptness, in either of two ways. Perhaps we fall short because, although we presuppose that the light is good, in appropriate conditions for doing so, nevertheless, our correctness still cannot be credited to our default competence, in its proper conditions. Given the jokester's presence, we might too easily so presuppose, in such conditions, and still get it wrong. Alternatively, we fail because the conditions for the exercise of our default competence are already spoiled by the very presence of the jokester. Either way, we then fail aptly to presuppose that the light is good, since we fail to presuppose correctly *through* the exercise of a competence in its appropriate conditions.

Is the case of ordinary perception alike in those crucial respects? That is not so clear. Among the things we must take for granted in attaining ordinary perceptual knowledge is that we are awake. What is our basis if any for so presupposing? Is it simply our being conscious? Plausibly it is, at least on the orthodox conception of dreams. In our dreams we are awake, and on the orthodox conception we thereby believe accordingly, while we dream. Plausibly, then, our basis when we take ourselves to be awake is simply being conscious. And what are the conditions appropriate for the exercise of this competence? Here it is less clear what to say.

Do we retain when dreaming our normal competence to tell when we are awake? No, sleep would seem to deprive us of normal competence to discern features of our experience that would show to someone awake that it was just a dream (if it is possible to inspect the contents of a dream while awake, which seems implied by the phenomenon of lucid dreaming).[5] Again, Austin spoke of a "dreamlike" quality, and Descartes of a certain lack of coherence. Suppose the orthodox conception is right, so that in dreaming we have real experiences, and respond to them with real beliefs, including the belief that one is awake. Perhaps we take for granted that we are awake whenever we are conscious. If our basis for so assuming is just being conscious, then the pertinent competence might too easily lead us astray in any ordinary situation, since in any ordinary situation, despite the proximity of the dream possibility, we would still assume ourselves to be awake on the same basis: namely, that of being conscious.

If we reason thus, however, we must then take back our claim that we can know ourselves to be in pain when we suffer excruciating pain, even if, through priming or hypochondria, we might easily have believed ourselves to suffer pain while it was only discomfort. We must take back that claim to know, for we can no longer claim the excruciating pain to be the relevant basis for our belief. After all, we would have believed ourselves to be in pain whether the pain had been

---

[5] Some competences are fundamental and minimally dependent on the episodic states of the subject. Others are more superficial, and dependent on the shape that the subject is in at the time. Intemperate drinking, for example, can reduce or remove one's competence to drive a car.

excruciating or not. So the real basis for the belief is some more determinable experience of which excruciating pain is only one determinate.

Suppose we resist such reasoning. Despite the fact that we would have believed ourselves in pain even when suffering only discomfort, we might argue, still there is some sense in which the excruciating pain is in all its intensity a cause and a basis of our belief that we are in pain. If so, then we open the way for a similar response to the problem of dreams. "Even if we would have believed ourselves awake had we simply been conscious," we could now say, "this does not take away the richer basis that we enjoy in waking life for the belief that one is awake." Now we could appeal, with Austin, to the vividness and richness of wakeful experience, and with Descartes to its coherence, as part of the basis for our belief that we are awake.

Of course, it may be that dreams pose a problem for the safety of ordinary perceptual knowledge in two ways. First, the phenomenological content of dreams may simply be different from that of waking life, in the ways suggested by Austin and Descartes.[6] So, the dreams you commonly

---

[6] Compare J. L. Austin's *Sense and Sensibilia* (Oxford: Oxford University Press, 1962), pp. 48–9: "I may have the experience (dubbed 'delusive' presumably) of dreaming that I am being presented to the Pope. Could it be seriously suggested that having this dream is 'qualitatively indistinguishable' from *actually being* presented to the Pope? Quite obviously not. After all, we have the phrase 'a dream-like quality'; some waking experiences are said to have this dream-like quality, and some artists and writers occasionally try to impart it, usually with scant success, to their works. But of course, if the fact here alleged *were* a fact, the phrase would be perfectly meaningless, because applicable to everything. If dreams were not 'qualitatively' different from waking experiences, then *every* waking experience would be like a dream; the dream-like quality would be, not difficult to capture, but impossible to avoid. It is true . . . that dreams are *narrated* in the same terms as waking experiences: these terms, after all, are the best terms we have; but it would be wildly wrong to conclude from this that what is narrated in the two cases is *exactly alike*. When we are hit on the head we sometimes say

undergo may very rarely if ever really be intrinsically much like wakeful experience in content. Second, being asleep may impair your competence to discern features relevant to whether it is a dream or waking life. So, the way in which you tell things in a dream—as when in dreaming you implicitly assume that you are awake and perceiving things—is not the competent way in which you do so in waking life. This may be because you do not have the same experiential basis, since the dream basis would fall short in respect of vividness, richness, or coherence. Alternatively,

that we 'see stars'; but for all that, seeing stars when you are hit on the head is *not* 'qualitatively' indistinguishable from seeing stars when you look at the sky."

Compare also the last paragraph of Descartes' *Meditations*: "I know that in matters regarding the well-being of the body, all my senses report the truth much more frequently than not. Also, I can almost always make use of more than one sense to investigate the same thing; and in addition, I can use both my memory, which connects present experiences with preceding ones, and my intellect, which has by now examined all the causes of error. Accordingly, I should not have any further fears about the falsity of what my senses tell me every day; on the contrary, the exaggerated doubts of the last few days should be dismissed as laughable. This applies especially to the principal reason for doubt, namely my inability to distinguish between being asleep and being awake. For I now notice that there is a vast difference between the two, in that dreams are never linked by memory with all the other actions of life as waking experiences are. If, while I am awake, anyone were suddenly to appear to me and then disappear immediately, as happens in sleep, so that I could not see where he had come from or where he had gone to, it would not be unreasonable for me to judge that he was a ghost, or a vision created in my brain [. . . like those that are formed in the brain when I sleep; (added in the French version)], rather than a real man. But when I distinctly see where things come from and where and when they come to me, and when I can connect my perceptions of them with the whole of the rest of my life without a break, then I am quite certain that when I encounter these things I am not asleep but awake. And I ought not to have even the slightest doubt of their reality if, after calling upon all the senses as well as my memory and my intellect in order to check them, I receive no conflicting reports from any of these sources. For from the fact that God is not a deceiver it follows that in cases like these I am completely free from error. But since the pressure of things to be done does not always allow us to stop and make such a meticulous check, it must be admitted that in this human life we are often liable to make mistakes about particular things, and we must acknowledge the weakness of our nature."

and compatibly, it may be because even if your experience in a dream could match ordinary waking experience in those respects, nevertheless your competence to take such respects into account would be so impaired when asleep that it would not matter. You would take yourself to be awake so long as you were conscious, regardless of how vivid, rich, or coherent your experience might or might not be.

Neither dream-involving threat to the safety of our perceptual beliefs is a threat to their aptness, however, since both would endanger only our normal competence to form perceptual beliefs. And we have seen how this can leave aptness unaffected.

The first lecture proposed an imagination model of dreams, as a way to block the skeptic's conclusion that dreams endanger ordinary perceptual beliefs. A further argument was still required for the further claim that our perceptual beliefs do normally rise above the animal level to a higher reflective level. And this led to a surprising pairing of our knowledge that we are awake with our knowledge of the *cogito*.

This second lecture proposes a virtue epistemology that distinguishes between aptness and safety of performance generally, and of belief in particular, which enables a further solution to the problem of dreams, beyond the imagination model. On this supplementary solution, dreams preclude the safety of our perceptual beliefs, but not their aptness, which is all they need in order to constitute animal knowledge.

In summary, some skeptics find a paradox at the heart of common sense. They argue that to know something requires that you believe it sensitively, in that had it been false you would not have believed it; or at least that you believe it on a basis such that had it been false you would not so believed it. A first step in response is to replace any such sensitivity requirement with one of safety, which a belief satisfies by having a basis that a belief would likely have only if it were right. A belief can thus be safe without being sensitive, which comports with the fact that subjunctive conditionals do not contrapose. Though more adequate than the sensitivity requirement, this requirement of safety is still inadequate. For we still face the skeptic's paradox, given that dreams are a common enough fact of life, unlike the usual run of outlandish skeptical scenarios. The special threat from dreams is that they seem to render our ordinary perceptual beliefs unsafe. Too easily might we have so believed on a similar enough basis in a dream, while our belief was false.

I have offered two ways to meet this threat. First, I contend in the first lecture that dreams do not contain real beliefs, and hence do not threaten the safety of our ordinary perceptual beliefs. Second, I propose in this second lecture a move beyond requiring that a belief must be safe in order to amount to knowledge, to a requirement of aptness rather than safety.

Consider indeed performances generally, not just intellectual performances such as judgments or beliefs. Your pertinent skill or competence, and your relevant situation for its exercise, can both be sufficiently fragile to render your performance unsafe, while it remains an apt performance nonetheless, one creditable to you as an attainment. Knowledge is simply such apt performance in the way of belief. Knowledge hence does not require the safety of the contained belief, since the belief can be unsafe owing to the fragility of the believer's competence or situation.[7]

---

[7] Consider the kind of simulation that a fighter pilot may have to go through. The pilot may well find himself in a situation that to him, strapped in as he is,

When we sleep and dream, then, our situation is in-appropriate for the manifestation of perceptual competence. Hence, even assuming that we do have perceptual beliefs in our dreams, these are not then apt beliefs, since even if and when they accidentally hit the mark of truth, they fail to do so in a way creditable to the believer's competence. But this does not affect the aptness of our perceptual beliefs in waking life.

In conclusion, animal knowledge is best viewed as apt belief, which enables a resolution of our skeptical paradox. As a bonus, it enables also a solution, at least in part, for the Gettier problem, the problem that beliefs can be true and justified without being knowledge. Our solution is that beliefs can be true and justified without being apt, whereas in order to constitute knowledge a belief must be apt, not just true and justified.

---

turns out to be indistinguishable from real life flying and shooting, even though it is only simulation. Given the nearness of such possibilities for a pilot as he nears the end of his period of training, how do we assess his real life flying and his good shots in those stages of his training, where simulation alternates with real flight. How good the pilot is will be assessed in part by reference to how easily he could now miss. And what is to be taken into account in determining this? Should we take into account that when the pilot now takes a real shot as he flies a real plane, he might too easily be in an indistinguishable simulation wherein he would go through what would seem to him to be real shots, though obviously no real target would be hit? How plausible can that be? Surely what matters is how remote the possibilities are wherein he takes a real shot in relevantly similar circumstances and still misses. There is a nearby possibility wherein he acts in a way that to him is indistinguishable from that of taking a real shot although he "misses" in the sense that no real target is hit. But this possibility seems irrelevant to evaluating how good a shot that pilot is now, and how good his real shots are. And an analogous point must now be considered concerning the thinker who shoots his answers at a certain range of questions. What affects how good an intellectual, epistemic shot that thinker is, and the epistemic quality of his actual beliefs? It is now in doubt that any possible situation wherein the thinker takes his shot and misses is automatically relevant to his pertinent evaluation and to the risk of error in his actual shot, if it is a situation that he cannot distinguish from the actual situation wherein he takes that shot.

That solution is partial since so far it deals with animal knowledge only, but it can be extended to cover also the sort of knowledge that requires reflective and apt endorsement of one's animal knowledge. It may indeed be thought that dreams still pose a problem for our claims to *reflective* perceptual knowledge. But we have seen the resources available to us for meeting also this deeper skepticism.

The fifth lecture will aim to deepen our solution to the problem of dreams based on distinguishing apt belief, or animal knowledge, from apt belief aptly noted, or reflective knowledge. The ways in which our virtue-based solution goes beyond the imagination model will then emerge more fully. Meanwhile, the two intervening lectures will use our aptness-centered epistemology to illuminate, first, the nature and epistemic role of intuitions, and, second, epistemic normativity and the problem of how knowledge can be better than mere true belief.

Lecture 3

Intuitions

Our topic is the nature and status of intuitions and intuitive justification, as they figure in a priori knowledge: in arithmetic, for example, or geometry. Three models will be compared: first, the traditional, perceptual model; second, the Cartesian, factive model; third, the competence or virtue model. I will argue against the first two, and in favor of the third.

Intuitions are found already in Platonic dialectic, with its ubiquitous use of the counterexample, and in ancient paradoxes: the liar, say, or the sorites, or the statue and the lump.

Intuitions are also important in contemporary philosophical debates: on names and reference, for example; on externalism vs. internalism in philosophy of mind and in epistemology; on the definition of knowledge, the nature of personal identity, essentialism . . . ; the list goes on. Relevant examples abound: trolley cars, split brains, Matrix scenarios, fake barns, Twin Earth; and so on.

What then *are* intuitions? What is their relevance to epistemic justification and knowledge? In addressing these questions, let's bear in mind two points:

1. First, we are interested in distinctively *epistemic* justification, not in pragmatic or any other sort of justification of beliefs or other attitudes. (Athletes and hospital patients derive practical benefits important enough to justify

their confidence. Assured confidence of success may even be pragmatically justified when the evidence goes, on balance, decidedly against it.)

2. Second, intuitions are supposed to play a *foundational* role in philosophy and other a priori disciplines (to the extent that these *are* a priori). They are supposed to provide justification relevantly independent of any reasoning, memory, perception, testimony, etc.[1]

What, again, are intuitions? Visual perception inspires the traditional model, with its "eye of the mind," and its "light of reason, or of nature." Consider an example:

Belief that here is a fire.

Experience as if one (directly) sees that here is a fire.

The fact that here is a fire.

---

[1] Putting aside memory and testimony, to the extent that these are channels conveying information and justification without generating it, foundational justi-fication is justification of an attitude that does *not* derive from its being based on a reason, on some other appropriate state of the subject's at the time, except insofar as the reason is not a state of the subject's that itself requires justification. So, my belief that I am in pain can be foundationally justified despite being based on a reason, but only because that reason, the pain itself, is not something that requires (or indeed admits) justification. (A state of one's own can of course provide justification to one's belief that one is in that state, without depending for this on its own justification, as when conscious belief that p helps justify belief that one consciously believes that p without this depending at all on the epistemic status of the belief that p. Here I will ignore this complication as a special case to be dealt with in a later refinement.) Is the pain a reason *why* but not a reason *for which*? I doubt it; when I am aware that my headache is starting, I have a reason *for* so believing, namely, that it is indeed starting. I am responding to my experience with an appropriate belief, and there is a reason within my consciousness why I so believe, *and for which* I so believe, by contrast to the neurological reasons *why* I so believe without believing for those reasons. It is surely relevant that I can make my reason explicit in the first case, with no need to rely on special empirical inquiry, but not so in the second case. In one case through introspective attention I can avow my reason for thinking that I am in pain, by saying that I so believe *because* I *am* in pain. Not so in the second case.

Here a visual experience mediates between the fact seen and the perceptual belief through which it is known. Experiences are able to provide justification that is foundational because they lie beyond justification and unjustification. Since they are only passively received, they cannot manifest obedience to anything, including rational norms, whether epistemic or otherwise. Since unmotivated by reasons, they can serve as *foundational* sources, as regress-stoppers. When they help explain the rational standing of some other state or action, they do *not* thereby problematize their *own* rational standing. Being so passive, they *have* no such standing.

Compare a case of rationally intuitive arithmetical knowledge:

Belief that $1 + 1 = 2$.

??

The fact that $1 + 1 = 2$.

No mediating state of awareness seems here to yield foundational justification, which conflicts with the perceptual model. Defenders of the model respond by distinguishing between two sets of examples:

$<3 + 2 = 5>$.

$<$A square has four sides$>$.

Instances of DeMorgan's Laws.

Instances of Double Negation.

The fact that $27 \times 323 = 8721$.

The Pythagorean Theorem.

The first set contains facts intuited, whereby the subject sees directly that things are thus and so. Facts in the second set, by contrast, must be proved in order to be known. How is our knowledge of the first set possible with no dependence on proof, nor even on any reasoning properly so-called?

According to the perceptual model, rational intuition would fit the following pattern:

Belief that $1 + 1 = 2$.

Intellectual seeming that $1 + 1 = 2$.

The fact that $1 + 1 = 2$.

Intellectual seeming is here seen as a state of awareness with a mediating role analogous to that of visual experience in visual perception.

Compare any familiar perceptual illusion: the Müller-Lyer, say, where opposing arrows make two congruent lines look incongruent. One's visual appearance or experience of incongruence turns out to be illusory. This for the perceptual model is akin to the apparent truth of a propositional content in a paradoxical cluster, as when it very much seems as if the successor of any small number must itself be small.[2]

Intellectual seemings are thus crucial to the perceptual model. What *are* these seemings? It is helpful to compare deliberation on a choice or the pondering of a question, where we "weigh" reasons pro or con. Switching metaphors, we feel the "pull" of conflicting considerations. No matter the metaphor, the phenomenon itself is familiar to us all.

---

[2] There are also linguistic illusions of grammaticality, such as perhaps the following (which I owe to Louise Antony): "More people have been to Paris than I have."

There is something it is *like* to feel the pull of contrary attractions as we deliberate or ponder.

Such intellectual seemings, such pulls, are distinct from *sensory* experiences. When we view a complex scene, a manifold spreads on our visual field, displaying complex characters that we *could* notice, and could even describe in words. But the display is there, so characterized, even before we notice its character, which we may never detail fully. The visual experience itself can have its own highly specific character *even* when it *attracts* no corresponding belief.[3]

Recall what we seek to understand: namely, how it is that intuitions could provide *foundational* justification, which must be direct, not inferential. According to classical

---

[3] Given that fact, indeed, one might wonder whether the Müller-Lyer visual experience is really one of incongruence. The lines on the page are of course equal in length. How about the lines in the mental visual field? The lines in one's image do not seem to change in length as congruent parallel lines are inserted sequentially between the two, or as vertical parallel lines are inserted, until the end points at one end are connected to those at the other end, which removes the appearance of incongruence. The lines *in one's visual field* are hence arguably congruent even before the new lines are inserted. In that light, the misleading "appearance" of incongruence may amount to a misled and misleading *intellectual seeming* rather than a sensory appearance. We are initially attracted to think the lines incongruent by the initial pattern, which contains just the two lines, but we are no longer so attracted by the final pattern, with its inserted lines, even though the two initial lines themselves are congruent all the while, from the initial visual field to the final one. What changes is just the attraction, so it is only in this sense that they initially "seem" incongruent, but congruent in the end.

Intellectual seeming also promises a way of understanding "seeing as," duck/rabbit phenomena. While the perceptual experience is determined by the lines on the page, and remains stable, we switch between conscious attraction to think the figure rabbit-like and conscious attraction to think it duck-like; however, the attraction has to be prompted by the perceptual experience directly, in a perceptual way. (After all, even when we see it as a duck, not a rabbit, we know that the figure before us, with a geometric pattern of lines just like this one, does look rabbit-like, though it does not at that very moment happen to be looking that way, since one has switched from the rabbit look to the duck look.)

foundationalists, we need a mental state that provides justification without requiring it in turn. For if it did itself
require it, then we would not have stopped the regress of
justifications, would not have found a foundational source.

Recall our perceptual example:

Belief that here is a fire.

Intellectual seeming that here is a fire.

Visual experience as if here is a fire.

The fact that here is a fire.

Such visual experience is thought to yield foundational justification, being itself beyond relevant evaluation, beyond
justification and unjustification. The intellectual seeming, by
contrast, *is* thus evaluable. A reason can be assigned the wrong
weight, as it attracts one's assent too much, or too little.

Intellectual seemings are especially dubious foundational sources once all-things-considered, resultant seemings are
distinguished from one-thing-considered, *prima facie* seemings. Prima facie seemings are *relative*: relative to the look of
Müller-Lyer lines, for example, one is prima facie attracted to
think them incongruent, while the result of a measurement
attracts one to the opposite conclusion. All-things-considered
seemings are *ultima facie*, or resultant seemings.

It is *resultant* intuitive seemings that most directly justify
corresponding intuitive beliefs. But we first consider intuitive
seemings that are not resultant but prima facie. These involve
a distinctive direct attraction to assent, one not motivated
through any train of reasoning, or any testimony, or perception, etc., not even through the channel of memory. How
do we understand this? *What*, more specifically, attracts us

when we are *thus* directly attracted? A plausible response is in line with long tradition: an attraction is intuitive or direct when it is exerted by the bare *understanding* of the proposition involved. But this would be an episodic grasping, an entertaining or having before the mind of that proposition. Plausibly, this is a determinable propositional attitude, whose determinates are more specific attitudes, such as occurrent belief, desire, etc. When it prevails against cognitive forces to the contrary, such attraction is promoted from being only prima facie to being a resultant, all-things-considered attraction.

A distinction is now required between two sorts of foundational justification: the basis-dependent and the competence-dependent, these being distinct though not mutually exclusive. A foundational source of epistemic justification for a propositional attitude must involve no further conscious rational basis, except only for foundational sources involving conscious bases that require no justification in turn. If a propositional attitude is to be foundationally justified, any conscious state on which it is rationally based must lie beyond justification and unjustification.[4]

> *Basis-dependent foundational justifi cation* is foundational justification that derives essentially from the justified belief's being based on a given state, a psychological state of the subject's, one that lies beyond justification and unjustification.

In hosting a certain attitude you are foundationally justified in the basis-dependent way to the extent that you are thus

---

[4] Or at least the state must provide its justification to the attitude without depending on its own justification for doing so, in line with the refinement specified earlier, in n.1 of Lecture 3.

justified through basing your attitude on a psychological state that lies beyond justification and unjustification.

Among sources of foundational justification that need not involve any basing, one will be of special interest to us:

> *Virtue foundational justification* is foundational justification that derives essentially from the justified propositional attitude's manifesting an epistemic competence.

In holding a certain belief you are foundationally justified in the virtuous way to the extent that you are then justified because in so believing you manifest a certain epistemic competence, one that is *not* constituted by your basing a belief on some other conscious state/reason for which you so believe.[5]

Intuitive intellectual seemings cannot provide basis-dependent *foundational* justification, being themselves epistemically evaluable. In general, again, a consideration can be assigned the *wrong* weight, as it attracts one too strongly or too weakly. Why should *intuitive* attractions be any exception? The sheer considering of a proposition can attract too much, if for example its attraction derives from enculturation into an unfortunate bias or superstition. I mean the kind of enculturation that works silently on the growing child, bypassing normal cognitive mechanisms of proper inference, testimony, or perception. One might thus end up giving a proposition the *wrong* intuitive weight: maybe it should hold no attraction whatsoever absent support by some good enough reason.

Does improper enculturation really work that way? Perhaps an initial attraction is exerted not just by one's considering the

---

[5] An illuminating question by Earl Conee led me to this distinction. All basis-dependent foundational justification might be virtue foundational, even while some virtue foundational justification is not basis-dependent.

unfortunate content, but rather by whatever social influence may instill the prejudice (with memory then preserving the attraction)? Such enculturation would be analogous to a combination of perception and memory. Often a visual experience as if p attracts us to believe that p, and this belief is then stored in memory long after we forget how it was first acquired. But this is not how enculturation works, at least not the sort invoked here. The relevant difference may be seen through a distinction between two kinds of attraction: that which is reason-based, and that which is not. The mechanisms of silent enculturation exert their influence in the second way, nonrationally, not through the operation of reasons, however cogent.[6]

What does the distinction amount to? Can this be specified more clearly? Reasons for one's attraction to assent to a proposition can take any of several forms. First, the *reason why* one is attracted might work through some causal mechanism not involving motives: through brainwashing, perhaps, or hypnosis, or some form of enculturation that is not reason-based. Second, a reason for one to be thus attracted might be accessible but not yet accessed. Neither of these is of main interest here. We focus rather on the mental states that motivate one to hold a certain attitude to a certain proposition, even a weak prima facie attraction. The reasons of interest for our discussion are those that might play a direct motivating role in the proper formation of belief, and these would be psychological states of the believer.

---

[6] Please bear in mind that the "rational" influence in play here is not always appropriate and justified. After all, the enculturation may result in a kind of reason-based attraction that is unjustified, where the reason-based attraction exerted by the sheer understanding of the proposition is misplaced. We avoid a dangerous ambiguity, therefore, if we use a terminology of "reason-based" rather than "rational" influence.

A more adequate picture must include the complication that some attractions are reason-based not directly but through memory. So, an attraction can remain reason-based while now stored in memory, if it was initially acquired on a rational basis, even if that basis is now forgotten. But there is no such basis in cases of brainwashing, or hypnosis, or enculturation that is not reason-based. And this is why there can be bad attraction that is still intuitive, since the *rational motivator* of one's attraction, the *motivating reason* why one is attracted (no matter how far back we go) is nothing more than the sheer understanding of that proposition, *with its specific content*, a *poor* reason at best in many cases of enculturation.

Here's another way to put the point: in such cases, my *rational basis* for attraction to assent to the propositional content lies in nothing more than my conscious entertaining of that content. There is no better response to the query as to the rational basis of my attraction, as to the reason *for which* I am thus attracted than something like this: because of what seems to me to be the fact that p. And this amounts to saying that it is merely the presence of the propositional content to my consciousness that is exerting the attraction, by being thus present, since nothing more than the propositional content is available to "seem to me to be the fact that p," not if it is false that p, so that there is no fact there to exert the rational attraction.

More naturally, it is true, one would respond to the query by saying: because of the fact that p. My more cautious suggestion reflects the fact that ignorance must be distinguished from irrationality. One can reach a certain judgment, for example, based on some supportive belief, even if, despite one's flawless rational performance, this belief turns out to be false. In that case one still has some reason for judging as one does, some reason that presumably involves one's supporting belief. Suppose one's judgment is based on a supporting belief that q. Since it is now supposed to be false that q, one would speak falsely if one cited as one's reason just the fact that q. I see no better way to protect one's rationality, and one's rational basis, against this untoward outcome, than to say that, even if it is false that q, so that one's reason cannot be the *fact* that q, one's reason might still perfectly well be what one *takes* to be the fact that q. And the same goes, *mutatis mutandis*, when we seek a rational basis, not for a full-fledged judgment, but only for an initial attraction.

In successful perception one is attracted to assent by a pre-attraction visual experience that foundationally explains one's prima facie justification for "taking that experience at face value," and for a corresponding belief. The perceptual prima facie attraction then properly prevails, becoming a resultant attraction, one strong enough to entail belief.

We can now better appreciate why that is an inadequate model for successful intuition. We have found intuitions to be best understood as intellectual seemings or attractions, and these, unlike visual experiences, are not factors *that attract us to assent* (whether the *facie* be *prima* or *ultima*). They are rather the attractions themselves. When such attraction is exerted by one's entertaining a proposition, with its specific content, then the attraction is intuitive. But the entertaining is not the intuition, not what is distinctively characteristic of *intuitive* justification. After all, conscious entertaining is always there in conscious belief, even when the belief is not intuitive, but introspective, perceptual, or inferential. What is distinctive of intuitive justification is rather *its being the entertaining itself of that specific content that exerts the attraction*. So, intuitions are attractions of a certain sort, with no rational basis beyond the conscious grasp of its specific propositional content.

What *intuitive* justification lacks is any correlate of the visual sensory experience beyond one's conscious entertaining of the propositional content, something that distinctively exerts a thereby justified attraction to assent. No such state of awareness, beyond the conscious entertaining itself, can be found in *intuitive* attraction.

Only one conclusion seems in order: that intuitions, unlike visual experiences, are *not* states of awareness that lie *beyond justification and unjustification*, able thereby to provide foundational justification while halting the regress of justification.

Have we perhaps looked in the wrong place for the foundationally justifying state of awareness? Perhaps in intuitive justification it is just the conscious entertaining itself that is the relevant state of awareness? No, there is a crucial difference between conscious entertaining and visual experiencing: if we visually experience that p (or as if p), we are thereby plausibly justified in our attraction to assent to <p> relative to that visual experience.[7] And the same is true for contents generally. By contrast, it would be ludicrous to suggest that consciously entertaining any given proposition prima facie justifies attraction to it. Only a very restricted set of propositions properly attract assent upon consideration, but we have been offered no clue as to the identity of that set.[8]

---

[7] Or so we are told by classical foundationalists, though they face the Speckled Hen problem, whose best solution would lead us in the epistemology of perception towards the same final destination as we will here be led in the epistemology of intuition, to an account based on competence rather than the mythological given.

[8] It might be suggested that any proposition entertained does thereby gain some prima facie justification, however minimal. The suggestion seems quite implausible, but we need not deny it outright in any case, if we switch our focus to differential justification, saying that what is distinctive of intuitive justification of a propositional content is that entertaining it justifies acceptance of it beyond what entertaining its negation would do for its negation.

(So we can explain such foundational justification by appeal neither to understanding in general, nor to understanding of propositional contents that meet some specified condition.)

That is why the perceptual model is inadequate for rationally intuitive knowledge or justification, which prompts us to consider an alternative. We turn next to the Cartesian model.

In explaining what it is to perceive clearly and distinctly, Descartes does not turn simply to logic, or arithmetic, or geometry. In his most prominent explanation of the notion,[9] he appeals rather to introspection. Even if our awareness that we suffer a pain has some clarity in it, we fall short of clear *and distinct* perception until we separate the hypothesis as to the origin of our feeling of pain from the perception that we have that feeling. It is the perception of the *feeling*, so detached, that attains both clarity and distinctness. So, Descartes' model of a kind of intuitive justification and knowledge is introspection, not perception. On this model there is no "eye of the mind" (though, at some expense of coherence, the "light of nature" is retained).

Here is the model at work in a specific example:

Belief that it hurts.

Intellectual seeming that it hurts.

The fact that it hurts.

On this "direct grasp" model, the fact that $1+1 = 2$ itself exerts its own attraction to the attentive mind. So, the corresponding example of intuitive justification and knowledge would look as follows.

---

[9] In his *Principles of Philosophy*, Principles 45 and 46.

Belief that $1+1 = 2$.

Intellectual seeming that $1+1 = 2$.

The fact that $1+1 = 2$.

According to this model, a propositional content about a present state of consciousness can attract assent through its sheer truth (though presumably it needs to be simple enough as well). Analogously, what properly draws your assent to propositional contents about simple arithmetic, geometry, and logic, is again their truth. And the corresponding belief may then be said, by extension, to be intuitively and even foundationally justified. One is justified intuitively by grasping a fact directly.

One problem is shared by this appeal to truth with the earlier appeal to understanding, for truth per se is no less ludicrous as a source of justification than is understanding per se, yet no condition has been specified that in combination with truth would plausibly explain foundational justification.

In addition, a further problem arises more specifically for the Cartesian model: namely, that there are *false* intuitively justified attractions, as in a powerful paradox, say the sorites. A paradox is a cluster of propositions all of which are intuitively attractive, powerfully so, though we are equally intuitively drawn to believe them jointly incoherent, or can be so drawn through simple reasoning. Before the paradox is discerned, our powerful attraction to any given member of the cluster is presumably justified, as is our corresponding belief. Inevitably, there will then be intuitively justified attraction to something false, and even intuitively justified false belief, perhaps belief eventually seen to be false once the paradox is resolved. That refutes the Cartesian model, which explains foundationally intuitively justified attractions and beliefs in terms of the *truth* of the contents involved, whereas in a paradox some attraction and its corresponding belief are intuitively justified without being true.

Descartes would have resisted this objection. The Cartesian response is instead to reject the problem, alleging that only real intuitions can justify. Something's *seeming* clear and distinct is on this view quite different from its *really being* clear and distinct. This Cartesian stance is surprisingly defensible through the epistemology of fallacious reasoning.

Suppose that, apart from having drawn it as a deductive conclusion, someone has no reason whatsoever for believing a certain proposition, one that can be known not directly but only through reasoning. If the reasoning is grossly fallacious, it cannot really justify the subject in believing that conclusion. When we work our way back through the reasoning we eventually hit the fallacy; let it be an affirming of the consequent. At that point it must have seemed intuitive to the reasoner to think something of the following form: *that, necessarily, if q, and p → q, then p.* In making that immediate inference, the thinker makes manifest his intuitive attraction to its corresponding conditional. But he cannot really be justified in being thus attracted to that conditional, nor in any corresponding belief. Whatever sort of epistemic justification he lacks for assenting to the conclusion is one he must also lack for attraction and assent to that unfortunate conditional. This reveals an advantage of the Cartesian account of intuition: that it explains our verdict about the fallacious intuition. Descartes suggests that the intuition at work in the fallacy is *apparent* intuition (*merely* apparent intuition), whereas only real intuition justifies. For him, all real intuition must be true, so the corresponding conditional of affirming the consequent cannot really be intuited. What is not a fact, on his view, is just not there to be intuited.

That is indeed a way to deal with the epistemology of falla-cious reasoning, but it is not the only way. Alternatively, what denies justification to the fallacious reasoner might just be his carelessness or inattention or blundering haste. With rare exceptions, normal, rational humans do not affirm the conse-quent when they are careful, attentive, and deliberate enough.

Similarly, if you know yourself to be relevantly color-blind, any color judgments you might venture would be unjustified, as they must be if they disregard the poor light, or the object's diminutive size, or how very far away it is. Contrast with this a judgment that is unreliable only because the lighting conditions are substandard in a way that the subject could not plausibly have suspected.

Fallacies can thus be viewed as performance errors charge-able against the subject, by contrast with deliverances of a competence. Unlike the Cartesian assimilation model, this account *can* admit the fallibility of intuition, can allow that paradox-enmeshed propositional contents exert proper attraction, on which one might even base justified intuitive belief. The attraction or belief is justified because it is compe-tent. Compare a perceptual illusion such as the Müller-Lyer. Before we know about the effect of the arrows, we are pow-erfully drawn to consider the lines incongruent, and may even believe accordingly with adequate justification. Only once we learn somehow that we are fooled by an illusion do we pull back from full assent. Our error is not just due to carelessness, moreover, nor to inattention or the like. No matter how good the light, no matter our psychological condition, or the qual-ity of our eyesight, we are inevitably subject to the illusion until we are relevantly clued in, even if we exercise utmost care and our attention is riveted. The attraction is a deliver-ance of our visual system itself, of the normal human visual system, which constitutes an indispensable competence for animals like us on the surface of our planet, one impressively reliable and productive, epistemically so.

That model is a worthy alternative to both the perceptual and the introspective models. By analogy to the seemings delivered by our visual system, the intuitions immediately delivered by our rational competences are preponderantly true, even if occasionally false. This is why those rational mechanisms are intellectual *competences*, because they systematically lead us aright. All seemings delivered by such competences are thereby epistemically justified.[10]

In sum, the proposed account has two parts: first, an understanding of intuitions as a special sort of intellectual seemings, *intuitive* seemings; second, a definition of the sort of intuition that is distinctively "rational."

1. An intellectual seeming is *intuitive* when it is an attraction to assent triggered simply by considering a proposition consciously with understanding. (Of course,

---

[10] Earlier we had put aside memory and testimony, to the extent that these are channels that convey information and justification without generating it, and had then tentatively adopted a characterization of foundational justification as an attitude's justification that does *not* derive from that attitude's being based on a reason, on some other state of the subject's at the time, except insofar as the reason is a state of the subject's that does not itself require justification. It fits with this characterization that attitudes not reason-based would qualify as foundationally justified if justified in virtue of how they derive from a competence. (I say "to the extent" that such channels convey justification without generating it for a reason: namely, that testimony-aided and memory-aided coherence does generate and not only convey some measure of justification, so in this way testimony and memory might be thought to participate essentially in the generation and not just the conveyance of justification. More plausibly, however, it is the coherence among already justified beliefs that boosts justification, so that memory and testimony are only indirectly relevant to the boost, and can still be viewed as chiefly conveyors of the epistemic goods.)

one may so much as understand the proposition only through a complex and prolonged process that includes perception, memory, testimony, or inference.)

2. S *rationally* intuits that p if and only if S's intuitive attraction to assent to <p> is explained by a competence (an epistemic ability or virtue) on the part of S to discriminate, among contents that he understands well enough, the true from the false, in some subfield of the modally strong (the necessarily true or necessarily false), with no reliance on introspection, perception, memory, testimony, or inference (no further reliance, anyhow, than any required for so much as understanding the given proposition).[11]

Let us take stock. Some of our knowledge plausibly has experiential foundations. When we know perceptually that p, we believe that p because it intellectually seems to us that p, all things considered. This in turn is so because it prima facie seems to us that p, and this prima facie seeming graduates into a resultant seeming because it prevails over any conflicting seemings that may bear on the matter. In such cases of empirical perception, what makes our prima facie attraction epistemically appropriate, finally, is that we experience sensorily as if p. And this last is not epistemically evaluable as something that you may be responsible for in a way that reflects on your reason-based cognitive processing,

---

[11] Jonathan Weinberg has quite properly questioned the restriction to the modally strong. And there is no very deep reason. This just seems the proper domain for philosophical uses of intuition. True, there are also *contingent* intuitions that derive from a competence. For example, there is a generic "taking experience at face value" competence. The intuitions that derive from this latter competence I prefer to call "animal intuitions," however, and these I would distinguish from the "rational" intuitions involved in abstract, a priori, armchair thought, of the kind we do in philosophy.

on your "reasoning," in a broad sense of this flexible term. Hosting that sensory experience at that time, with its specific character, is not constitutive of or directly due to your faculty of reason, nor is it in any way due to your reasoning. You do not experience that way motivated by a reason, you do not so experience *for* a reason that you have, one that *motivates* you to experience that way.

Something similar holds for introspective knowledge. When we know introspectively that p, it seems to us both *prima* and *ultima facie* that p, and this in turn has an explanation in a motivating mental state that we host. Thus, if I know introspectively that I am in pain, it is the pain itself that attracts me, both *prima* and *ultima facie*, to believe that I am in pain. And the pain itself is neither constitutive of the subject's rational faculties, nor in any way due to any "reasoning" on the subject's part. Moreover, the pain itself is of course not evaluable epistemically.

No such state beyond justification or unjustification seems available to serve as foundation for intuitive justification or knowledge. No distinctive experiential state serves here as a basis, as a motivating reason for attraction to assent. We find nothing like the sensory experience that prompts a perceptual belief or the pain that prompts an introspective belief. When we are intuitively justified in believing that p, we are attracted to so believe through the mere grasp of the content that p, which we then entertain. So, it is the mere entertaining of that very content that prompts attraction and perhaps assent.

However, we have found that such attraction can be evaluated epistemically and might in fact be most unfortunate, in which case it could hardly provide epistemic justification to any belief founded upon it. Only *competently* derived intuitive seemings could do so. And it is just this difference that makes the epistemic difference, that distinguishes the foundationally justified seeming, including the rational intuition.[12]

Objections and replies

Any argument for our account will face the objection that intuitions cannot properly support their own probative force, since any such argument is likely to depend on intuition at some point, if not in its premises, then at least in its transitions. This objection is in line with two prominent attacks on the use of intuitions in philosophy. First there is the "calibration" objection,[13] according to which an essential part of our basis for trusting intuitions is provided, viciously, by none other than just intuitions. Second, we face the objection that intuitions derive too much from mere enculturation to be systematically representative of the truth, as is shown by how extensively they clash across cultures and socio-economic groups.[14] We take up these objections in order.

---

[12] Of course, idiosyncratic seemings do not provide examples of *human* foundational justification, no matter how impressively competent, precisely because they are idiosyncratic and not humanly normal. But a Ramanujan can still enjoy superhuman and epistemically effective intuitions.

[13] See, e.g., Robert Cummins's "Reflection on Reflective Equilibrium," in M. DePaul and W. Ramsey (eds.), *Rethinking Intuition* (Lanham, MD: Rowman & Littlefield, 1998).

[14] This line of objection has been developed most impressively by Stephen Stich over the years, recently in collaboration with Jonathan Weinberg and Shaun Nichols. See Stephen Stich, "Reflective Equilibrium, Analytic Epistemology, and the Problem of Cognitive Diversity," *Synthese* 74 (1988): 391–413; also Jonathan Weinberg, Shaun Nichols, and Stephen Stich, "Normativity and Epistemic Intuitions," in *The Philosophy of Alvin Goldman*, a special issue of *Philosophical Topics* 29/1 and 2: 429–61, ed. Christopher S. Hill, Hilary Kornblith, and Thomas Senor; and Shaun Nichols, Stephen Stich, and Jonathan Weinberg,

The calibration objection, if effective against intuitions will prove a skeptical quicksand that engulfs all knowledge, not just the intuitive. No source will then survive, since none can be calibrated without eventual self-dependence. That is so at least for sources broadly enough conceived: as, say, memory, introspection, and perception. None of these can be defended epistemically as reliable enough unless allowed to yield some of the data to be used in its own defense.

Alternatively, we might distinguish among the various subfaculties of perception, allowing a distinction between vision and hearing, for example, so that the reliability of either could gain support by leaning on the other. There are two important points to consider in evaluating this approach.

First, we might support *either* by leaning on the other, but not *each* by leaning on the other. Without this more demanding result, however, we face the same calibration problem for perception as a whole.

Besides, second, if the "divide and conquer" strategy could somehow be made to work for perception, it could surely be adapted for the support of intuition. Thus, one could lean one's own intuitions evidentially on those of others. Or one could distinguish to similar effect between one's intuitions at a given time and those at another time. But this line of defense would lead eventually to the second main objection—that, across socio-economic or cultural divides, we find serious conflicts of intuition—to which we turn next.

"Meta-skepticism: Meditations in Ethno-epistemology," in S. Luper (ed.), *The Skeptics* (Aldershot: Ashgate, 2003). My take on the methodology used in these attacks, and on the results attained, is in "A Defense of Intuitions," forthcoming in *Stephen Stich and His Critics*, ed. Dominic Murphy and Michael Bishop (Oxford: Blackwell, 2007).

Merely verbal disagreement will cast no doubt on intuition. Why not say that across the divides different concepts are picked out by terminology that is either ambiguous or contextually divergent. Thus, on one side the more valuable epistemic status perhaps involves communitarian factors of one or another sort (factors that social psychologists and experimental philosophers have thought might distinguish East Asians from Westerners), factors absent from what the other side picks out as "knowledge." If there is such divergence in meaning, or contextual variation in reference, then once again there is here no disagreement on the very same propositions. In saying that the subject does not know, one side is saying something about lack of some relevant communitarian status. In saying that the subject does know, the other side is not denying that, but is simply focusing on a different status, one thought desirable even without meeting the communitarian requirements. The proposition affirmed by one side as intuitively true is not the very one denied by the other side as intuitively false.

Is there a real disagreement when one side insists on communitarian standards for the formation of beliefs while the other side does not? This raises an interesting question about the content of epistemic normative claims. When we say that a belief is justified, epistemically justified, or even amounts to knowledge, are we issuing a normative verdict that one *should* form or sustain that belief? Not plausibly: it might be an obvious waste of time to be forming a belief on that question. Are we even saying so much as this: that if we leave aside other desiderata proper to a flourishing life, and focus only on epistemic desiderata, then we should be forming or sustaining this belief? I doubt that our talk of knowledge and epistemic justification is properly understood along these lines.

One may out of the blue wonder how many coffee beans remain in one's coffee bag, a very careful count of which reveals that it contains n beans. Is this something that one *should* then believe? Well, in one clear sense it is *not*. Clearly one should not even concern oneself with that question, so it is false that one should be conducting one's intellectual life so as to return an affirmative answer to it. The whole question is beneath one's notice. One should not be forming *any* opinion on it, positive or negative. One has better things to do with one's time, even restricting ourselves to properly epistemic concerns.

One of our two conflicting ways to understand knowledge privileged communitarian factors. But it is now hard to see why that would require us to seek such beliefs, or to approve of such beliefs, or even to approve of such beliefs once we restrict ourselves to *epistemic* concerns. Silly beliefs about trivial matters can attain the very highest levels of justification and knowledge even if these are not beliefs that one should be bothering with, not *even if* one's concerns are purely epistemic. Even if the privileged communitarian factors are required in any belief that aspires to be knowledge, therefore, this does not imply that we should *ipso facto* seek such beliefs.

Thus, the supposed normativity of epistemology seems rather like the normativity of a *good* gun or a *good* shot. This normativity is restricted to the sphere of guns and shots in some way that isolates it from other important concerns, even from whether there should be guns at all, or shots. At least that seems clear for a discipline of epistemology whose scope is the nature, conditions, and extent of knowledge. If ours is the right way to understand such normativity, then in speaking of a justified belief we are saying something rather like "Good shot!" which someone might sincerely and correctly say despite being opposed to gun possession and to shooting.[15]

And now any vestige of conflict across the divides is in doubt. For now there seems no more conflict here than there is between someone who rates cars in respect of how economical they are and someone who rates them in respect of how fast they can go.

Beyond all such considerations, however, we must also acknowledge the sort of disagreement that divides the superstitious from the enlightened. The enlightened are not just saying that the superstitious value beliefs that satisfy certain conditions (derivation from tea leaves, or crystal balls, or certain writings) such that the enlightened are just focused on *different* conditions. No, the enlightened *object* to the conditions elevated by the superstitious. But they do not *necessarily* object to the formation of such beliefs as a means to inner peace or community solidarity. They *may* object this way too, but they *need* not, and probably *should* not, at least in some actual cases of primitive cultures, and in many conceivable ones. The enlightened deny that the sort of status elevated by the superstitious constitutes *epistemic* value in the actual world, for the reason, presumably, that it is insufficiently connected with truth.

Compare a culture that loves the way a certain sort of gun sounds, even though it is woefully unreliable and far inferior

---

[15] This leaves open the possibility of a broader concern with the *kind* of knowledge we should seek in a good life. Wisdom might be one such, something closely connected with how to live well, individually and collectively. Another such might be a world view that provides deep and broad understanding of major departments of proper human curiosity, which of course cries out for an account of what makes curiosity proper. Of course, certain *kinds* of knowledge might be valuable and highly desirable, without knowledge per se being so.

to bows and arrows. The visiting military advisor need not object to their preference for that sound, nor *need* he object to their taking the gun into battle in preference to their bows and arrows. He need not object to that *all* things considered. That would be at most the business of a political advisor; actually, not even he may be in a position to make any such all-things-considered objection.

The military advisor's advice is restricted to informing his clients on what would produce the best results in the battlefield *with regard to military objectives*. The political advisor's advice would take that into account, but would encompass also broader *political objectives*. And even that will not cover the full span of considerable objectives.

Something similar is true of epistemology. Epistemic justification concerns specifically *epistemic* values, such as truth, surely, and perhaps others not entirely reducible to truth, such as understanding.

Even once we put aside inner peace, happiness, solidarity, and technological control, as not properly *epistemic* values, however, various remaining statuses of a belief may still qualify as epistemic, such as the following:

- being true
- being a truth-tracker (would be held if true, not if not true)
- being safe (would not be held unless true)
- being virtuously based (derives from a truth-reliable source)
- being rationally defensible by the believer
- being reflectively epistemically defensible by the believer (rationally defensible in respect of the truth-reliability of its sources)

- being virtuously based through a virtue recognized as such in the believer's community (and, perhaps, *properly* recognized as such).

Interestingly enough, it is not just people from different cultures or different socio-economic groups who apparently diverge in rational intuitions on epistemic questions. Notoriously, contemporary analytic epistemologists have disagreed among themselves, though they are nearly all professors at colleges or universities, nearly all English-speaking Westerners. On one side are internalist, evidentialist, classical foundationalists; on the other externalists of various stripes: process reliabilists, trackers, proper functionalists, some virtue epistemologists. It is increasingly clear, and increasingly recognized, that the supposed intuitive disagreements across this divide are to a large extent spurious, that different epistemic values are in play, and that much of the disagreement will yield to a linguistic recognition of that fact, perhaps through a distinction between "animal" knowledge and "unreflective" justification, on one side, and "reflective" knowledge and justification on the other.

Both the calibration objection and the supposed cultural or socio-economic conflicts seem unpersuasive as they now stand.

The next lecture will attempt to deepen our understanding of the epistemic normativity recently broached.

Lecture 4

Epistemic Normativity

We humans are zestfully judgmental across the gamut of our experience: in art, literature, science, politics, sports, food, wine, and even coffee; and so on, across many other domains.[1] We love to evaluate even when no practical interest is in play. We judge performances, whether artistic or athletic; grade products of craft or ingenuity; evaluate attitudes, emotions, institutions, and much more.

Any such domain of human experience admits values of two sorts: the derivative, and the fundamental—that is to say, the derivative or fundamental *for that domain*. A value might be irreducible to other values distinctive of a given domain, without being fundamental absolutely, since reducible to other values *beyond* that domain.

According to epistemic truth monism, truth is the fundamental epistemic value.[2] The epistemic justification of a

---

[1] In a narrow, praxiological, sense, normativity pertains to choice or action, and to rules or standards for choosing or assessing conduct. In an extended, axiological, sense, it pertains to the evaluative more generally, whether the objects of evaluation be actions or not. The two are intimately related, since conduct that brings about something intrinsically good is to that extent apt, even if it must meet further requirements of rational control and intentional guidance. Here we take the broader view.

[2] One might defensibly define generic reliabilism as a truth-monistic view. But there are various equally defensible ways to understand that important, but flexible, epistemic term "reliabilism." On some of these, externalism is not crucial, and Descartes counts straightforwardly as an extreme, *infallibilist*, reliabilist.

belief, its epistemically positive status beyond that of being true, is held to involve truth-conducive reliability, however conceived, whether as tracking the truth, or as deriving from a reliable process, or competence, or virtue. A true belief is said to constitute knowledge only through some such connection with the truth.

In calling a belief knowledge, we evaluate it positively by epistemic standards. Within the domain of epistemic assessment, knowledge has a standing higher than that given to its constitutive belief by its mere truth. But how can this be, if truth is the fundamental epistemic value? Suppose a belief is epistemically justified if and only if it derives from a truth-reliable source, because what matters essentially and distinctively in epistemology is whether and how we are in touch with the truth. In that case, once true, a belief would seem to gain nothing further from being thus justified.

Our worry goes beyond the Platonic worry of how *knowledge* that a certain road leads to Larissa could be better than *true belief*, if either will get you there equally well. The Larissa worry is assuaged by a distinction between epistemic and pragmatic varieties of justification. The efficiency of our belief in getting us to Larissa is to be distinguished from its distinctively *epistemic* normative status. Knowledge could of course have a value beyond such efficiency. But the belief's epistemic status must then concern more than just how well it guides you to your objectives. Not even by restricting ourselves to *epistemic* objectives, such as that of gaining truths, can we reduce epistemic justification to instrumental value. You may lack justification for trusting a certain book, for example, even if it would reveal a trove of truths. This sort of epistemic efficacy does not even protect the belief that the book is trustworthy from being wildly unjustified. Despite overwhelming evidence that the book is not to be trusted, believing it trustworthy might still give you that trove of truths.

Our present worry abstracts from such Platonic issues of epistemic normativity. Truth may or may not be intrinsically valuable absolutely, who knows? Our worry requires only that we consider truth the *epistemically fundamental* value, the ultimate explainer of other distinctively epistemic values.

Our issue for truth-centered epistemology, beyond the Larissa problem, is the "value problem," as follows:

How can the truth-reliability of an epistemic source give to the beliefs that it yields any additional epistemic worth, over and above any that they already have in virtue of being *true*?[3]

Compare this. A cup of coffee is not a better cup of coffee for being yielded by a good, reliable machine! It will be useful here to compare (a) the realm of the epistemic, with (b) the world of coffee. Are these critical domains similarly structured? A tabular comparison is shown in Table 4.1.

---

[3] Our issues of epistemic normativity are discussed in a growing literature that includes the following early contributions: Ward E. Jones, "Why Do We Value Knowledge?," *American Philosophical Quarterly* 34 (1997): 423–39; Jonathan L. Kvanvig, "Why Should Inquiring Minds Want to Know? *Meno* Problems and Epistemological Axiology," *The Monist* 81 (1998): 426–51; Linda Zagzebski, "From Reliability to Virtue Epistemology," in G. Axtell (ed.), *Knowledge, Belief, and Character* (Lanham, MD: Rowman & Littlefield, 2000); Marian David, "Truth as the Epistemic Goal," in M. Steup (ed.), *Knowledge, Truth, and Duty* (Oxford: Oxford University Press, 2001); Michael DePaul, "Value Monism in Epistemology," in Steup, op. cit.; Wayne Riggs, "Reliability and the Value of Knowledge," *Philosophy and Phenomenological Research* 64(2002): 79–96. In the present lecture I develop an approach sketched in "Beyond Skepticism, to the Best of Our Knowledge," *Mind* (1988), and in "Reflective Knowledge in the Best Circles," *Journal of Philosophy* (1997), reprinted in Steup, op cit.

Table 4.1 Epistemic comparison

Epistemology	Coffee criticism
Beliefs	Liquid coffee
Concepts	Ground coffee, coffee beans, coffee makers
Believers and their ways of forming and holding beliefs	Baristas and their ways of making liquid coffee
Schools, modes and methods of teaching, laboratories, modes of inquiry, epistemic communities, criteria of assessment and promotion	Coffee plantations, harvests, ways of grinding, kinds of land, climate, relation to the sun, etc.
True beliefs and theories	Delicious, aromatic liquid coffee

Consider the world of coffee—of its production, elaboration, and consumption. One central value organizes the critical assessment distinctive of that domain. I mean the value of liquid coffee that is delicious and aromatic. Think of the assessment of coffee beans, fields, coffee machines, baristas, ways of making liquid coffee, plantations, harvests, etc. What organizes all such evaluation, the value at the center of it all, from which the other relevant values are derivative, is the value of good coffee, of liquid coffee that is delicious and aromatic. (We leave aside the use of coffee in recipes, liqueur, ice cream, etc.; these may also be fundamental, but they are peripheral.)'

The world of coffee is a "critical domain," a set of interrelated entities evaluable through correspondingly interrelated values. Paradoxically, one can be an adept critic within such a domain even while discerning in it no domain-transcendent value. Thus, someone knowledgeable about guns and their use for hunting, for military ends, and so on, may undergo a conversion that makes the use of guns abhorrent. The good shot is thus drained of any real value that he can discern. Nevertheless, his critical judgment within that domain may outstrip anyone else's, whether gun lover or not. Critical domains can be viewed as thus *insulated,* in ways suggested by our example.[4]

Instrumental value is among the kinds of value that derive from more fundamental values. When a barista does a "good" job, he does things that produce some good coffee. The barista does "well" because his actions result in the good coffee. But extrinsic value takes many other forms besides the instrumental. What makes for the goodness of good fields, for example, or good beans, good coffee makers, or good baristas, is not exactly their efficiently causing something good at the time when they are "good" exemplars of their kind. Nevertheless, efficient production of the fundamentally good is also implicated in these other varieties of goodness. Given its importance, not only on its own, but also in explaining other forms of evaluation, instrumental goodness deserves a closer look.

If your taking some aspirin relieves your migraine without side effects, then it is probably a good thing you do, good in virtue of its good effects, including the removal of the headache. Let's here assume that the relief is itself a good, so that the taking of the aspirin produces something good (or, if that is found implausible, suppose you down the pill with a good Scotch). On that assumption, let us now abbreviate as follows.

T = the taking of the aspirin (with the Scotch).

P = the pleasure produced.

When we say to the subject, about T, "that's a good thing you did," we base ourselves on what T brought about. What

---

[4] A chess master, such as Bobby Fischer, might become depressed and disenchanted with chess, while retaining his preeminence at the chessboard, and his peerless critical judgment.

made it a good thing to do is its causing something good, the relief (or pleasure) that ensues.

Compare now the following two facts:

The causal fact: <T produces P>.

The temporal fact: <T precedes P>.

Only the causal fact gives rise to a widely recognized, distinctive sort of value, the instrumental value that T inherits from it. The temporal fact does not bestow on T any recognized sort of value. But why should that be? Isn't it just arbitrary to distinguish thus between the causal relation and the temporal relation? Why not recognize a kind of "precedence value" related to the temporal fact as is instrumental value to the causal fact? Why not even allow a "coincidence" value that T can have through its mere *coexistence* with the valuable P?

Distinguishing instrumental value from these other definable forms of "value" is hardly arbitrary, surely, though we cannot stop now to detail why. For some reason, causation enters into the proper determination of values beyond the intrinsic in a way denied to mere precedence and coexistence. Causation helps induce other values, instrumental value prominent among them, in a way that mere temporal relations and bare coexistence are powerless to do.

Moreover, causation can work in either direction, by helping induce further value in a cause, or alternatively by helping induce further value in an effect, as in the following example.

A ballerina's body moves across a stage with utmost grace. We take great pleasure in those graceful movements; we admire and applaud them. Then we learn that the dancer was drugged, her movements mere stumbles, nothing more. How now do we assess what happened, however improbably, on that stage?

One might of course still admire the movements, as we admire the swelling flow of Niagara, or falling snow in bright sunlight, as natural phenomena with immediately appreciable beauty. Many would react that way. For others, the disappointment would be so great as to obscure any natural beauty to be found in the movements themselves, however produced, whether through artistic control or through stumbles. Why disappointment? What we had paid for, surely, was not just to see stumbles, however graceful. We had paid to see a performance, the product of artistic excellence and control. We take pleasure in seeing the grace of the movements, true enough, but we take special pleasure in knowing it to be grace due to the ballerina and, more particularly, to her art. It is her actions that we normally admire and value.

One and the same item does not in that example clearly gain a kind of value through how it is caused, however, just as the taking of the aspirin might or might not have a kind of value, instrumental value, depending on what it causes. In our example, causation plays a crucial role. It's the movements under the dancer's *control* that we admire. But it is not clear that causation is there adding value to something that might still have existed but would not have had that value without its causal liaison.

The plastic arts provide a better example. We come across a canvas in a museum and admire the design on it. What if the canvas turns out to be a patch covering a wall under repairs? What if the design got there when the canvas rubbed against something on the way to the wall? What if a still un-removed sign below the now removed painting had attributed the design to Picasso? Do we still value and admire that design just the same once we learn its true origin? Surely not, but what makes the difference?

It is not the action of Picasso painting a painting that we admire when we view a real Picasso, as we admire the ballerina's dance. The artist's action might be admired when he is seen at work in his studio. But it is not what we admire now as we view the painting in a museum. Nor do we admire the painting's having been painted by Picasso. Our admiration need not even grow much when we learn the artist's name and biographical profile.[5] What does normally matter is whether the design is owed to a mere accidental rubbing or to an artist's genius. What is valued, however, what is assessed as valuable, is the work of art itself, the painting, not the fact of its having been created by someone or other, someone whose identity we may not even know. What is admired is that design, those lines and colors on the canvas, not the fact that they were authored. Nevertheless, its origin does matter, as noted: an accidental rubbing, again, is not a work of art.

Something similar holds for epistemology. To begin, Table 4.2 compares two domains of normative criticism, one epistemic, one athletic.

The good shot is the central value that organizes the sport of archery and the criticism proper to it. Think of how we grade other things distinctive of the world of archery. All such evaluation is dependent on the value constituted by the good shot. Consider, for example, what determines the quality of bows, arrows, archers, archery schools, methods, training camps, and so on. This all depends on the value of the good shot, which is fundamental to

---

[5] The value of a painting *can* of course depend on its specific authorship. This is reflected in its market value.

Table 4.2 Comparison of two domains of normative criticism

Epistemology	Archery criticism
Beliefs	Shots
Concepts	Bows, arrows
Believers and their ways of forming and sustaining beliefs	Archers and their ways of shooting
Schools, methods of teaching, modes of inquiry. Epistemic communities, criteria for rating and promoting	Communities that preserve, supplement, and transmit the lore of archery, honoring accomplishment in accordance with criteria
True beliefs	Accurate shots
True beliefs might vary in epistemic respects; for example, some have more content than others, being more specific	Accurate shots might vary in respects relevant to archery; for example, some come closer to the bull's-eye than others

archery criticism, through the ways in which it is constitutive of other values proper to that field: the quality of bows, for example, or of arrows, archers, methods, etc.

Truth is similarly a fundamental value of epistemology. Evaluation is distinctively epistemic when it is concerned with truth. Granted, belief *is* pragmatically evaluable. Hospital patients and competitive athletes might be helped to prevail through confidence, which is thus well placed pragmatically, even when evidentially baseless.

A shot might be accurate without being adroit. It might hit the bull's-eye aided by a gust of wind without which it would have missed the target altogether. In that case, the shot is accurate though unskillful. Contrariwise, a shot might be inaccurate though skillful. Perhaps it would have hit the bull's-eye but for the gust that diverts it.

A shot is adroitly accurate, then, only if it is accurate while manifesting the archer's skill. This much is good as far as it goes, but it might still fall short. An archer might manifest sublime skill in a shot that does hit the bull's-eye. This shot is then both accurate and adroit. But it could still fail to be accurate *because* adroit. The arrow might be diverted by some wind, for example, so that, if conditions remained normal thereafter, it would miss the target altogether. However, shifting winds might then ease it back on track towards the bull's-eye. Though accurate and adroit, this shot would still fail to be "apt," that is to say, accurate *because* adroit.

Aptness depends on just *how* the adroitness bears on the accuracy. The wind may help some, for example; it may even help enough that the arrow would otherwise have bounced off the side of the target on its way to the ground. Only with the wind's help does it bury its tip near the bull's-eye. If the shot is difficult, however, from a great distance, the shot might still be accurate sufficiently through adroitness to count as apt, though with some help from the wind.

An index of sufficiency seems required, with some threshold, probably contextually determined, so that we can affirm this:

A shot is apt if and only if its accuracy is due "sufficiently" to the archer's adroitness.

What does such "sufficiency" depend upon? This is a difficult and interesting question that we must here postpone. Better yet, we might do well to abstract from the threshold-requiring classificatory concept to its presupposed comparative, as follows:

How apt a shot is varies in direct proportion to the adroitness manifest by the archer and to how much its accuracy is due to that adroitness.

Alternatively, we might understand success due to an agent's competence as success that *manifests* that competence, a special case of the manifestation of a disposition. But we cannot tarry over this promising alternative.

Epistemology too, like the aesthetics of dance, reverses the import of causality found in instrumental value. The distinctively epistemic evaluation of a cognitive performance can depend substantially on its source, unlike the instrumental evaluation that depends on effects rather than sources. Consider thus the justification of a belief derived from a good inference, as when a detective figures out who did it, or when you determine how much you owe a shopkeeper. Something is then believed because it is concluded from prior information already in the thinker's possession. To draw it as a conclusion and to believe accordingly for that reason is, moreover, a broadly causal matter. It is a matter of believing such and such *because* of so and so, or *on the basis* of a prior belief that so and so. Accordingly, the conclusion belief gains its epistemic status through being *based* on the premises inferentially. One believes the conclusion at least in part on that basis, *for the reason* that, as one can see, it follows from the already accepted information. The fact that one's belief in the conclusion is thus "motivated rationally" helps to make it epistemically appropriate, a rationally justified believing.

How must a belief be related to a fact if it is to be knowledge of that fact? According to one proposal, the belief must be safe, that is, one that the believer *would then hold only if correct*. A second proposal requires the belief to be apt, correct in a way creditable to the believer, as determined by how salient is the believer's competence in the explanation of his being right.

Although both conditions still seem defensible in some form,[6] each needs qualification. Although the right requirement in this vicinity is one of aptness, this is not to be explained just by appeal to explanatory salience, or to avoidance of luck or accident. The reasons emerge already with the problems canvassed earlier[7] for any unrestricted requirement of safety.

A virtuous performance, whether a correct belief due to intellectual virtue or a right action due to practical virtue, will involve both the agent's constitution and his situation. If the act is due to a competence exercised in its appropriate conditions, its success may be due to luck in various ways. It may be just an accident that the agent retains his relevant competence, for example, or that the conditions remain appropriate. Either way, the act fails to be *safely* successful, since it might too easily have failed, through lack of the required competence or conditions. It might still be apt, nevertheless, indeed attributably, creditably apt.

A certain archer's shot hits the mark through a normal exercise of skill, let us suppose, in normal circumstances. What if the archer might easily have been disabled, having just taken an unadulterated drink at random from a collection nearly all adulterated? What if a gust of wind or stroke of lightning *might easily* have denied him his propitious situation for part at least of the relevant period, by affecting the arrow on its way to the target? Even so, the shot might have been apt, surely, still accurate because adroit, and creditable to

---

[6] More recently the idea has been developed insightfully by John Greco; see his "Knowledge as Credit for True Belief," in Michael DePaul and Linda Zagzebski (eds.), *Intellectual Virtue: Perspectives from Ethics and Epistemology* (Oxford: Oxford University Press, 2004).

[7] In Lecture 2.

the agent, so long as the competence remained in place, and the conditions appropriate, even if only by luck. What matters is that the conditions remain appropriately normal (or better) along dimensions relevant to the agent's retained competence.

The same goes for any apt belief accurate due to the subject's competence. A belief can be unsafe because the subject might too easily become disabled, or because the conditions might too easily become inappropriate. Suppose you see a surface to be red, for example, by exercising your visual competence in good light. Perhaps you took an unadulterated drink at random, however, from amongst many containing a color-blinding drug. Or perhaps the surface might too easily have been lit with red light, making it impossible to see red patches in their true colors. In such circumstances, where too easily you might have lacked the requisite competence or conditions, your color belief would have been unsafe. Nonetheless, it might have been apt even so, still correct due to competence. Or so one would think, if the archer's shot can be apt despite clear and present threats to his competence, and to the appropriate normalcy of his situation.

Our reasoning distinguishes between (i) factors because of which the circumstances *might* now easily have failed to be normal, without *already* being abnormal, and (ii) factors that *do* already preclude normalcy. Factors of sort (i) make a belief unsafe without precluding its being apt, that is, correct because adroit. Factors of sort (ii) deprive the belief not only of safety but also of aptness.[8]

---

[8] More strictly, if the subject's performance is to be apt, then the conditions must be normal *or better*. But this requires a prior or at least coordinate conception of the relevant adroitness or skill or competence. What is required in the conditions is that they be normal or better *for the exercise of the relevant competence*.

Outright safety is not a requirement for apt performance in any case. A performance can still be apt when its safety depends on a circumstantial contingency, provided it is guided by that contingency. Even if the light alternates quickly and randomly between being bad and being good, one can still acquire perceptual knowledge so long as the deliverances of one's color vision are accepted, not just at face value, but guided by the ringing of a bell bound to ring steadily when and only when the light is good.

Think back, however, to the easily possible gust of wind or stroke of lighting, or to the lighting conditions that might easily have been spoiled. One's performance could then still be apt despite failing to be safe outright, since safe only dependently on a factor that might too easily have been absent. Here the agent's performance need not even be guided by the factor dependently on which it is apt. Question: what distinguishes such contingencies, those on which the performance can depend for its safety and aptness without benefit of guidance?

Our purposes in evaluating people plausibly help determine that distinction, given our need for coordination and mutual reliance, and hence for keeping track of strengths and weaknesses, our own and others'. We value, as "aptitudes," certain abilities relative to certain background conditions. Such abilities are relative to distinctive correlated parameters at the time of their exercise. That you have the ability means that your relevant performances tend to succeed when they fall within those parameters. This applies to athletic prowess, intellectual abilities, crafts, skills, and so on. Failed attempts

---

This is why the lucky gust does not make the conditions better than normal, enabling the archer to earn credit for a great shot. The gust creates conditions wherein it is not any skill manifest by the archer that is operative. The gust takes over independently of anything that could count as such a skill.

in abnormal circumstances do not show lack of the ability. Despite such failures we might still depend on you in normal circumstances. What is required is only that your attempts tend to succeed when circumstances are normal. (And the like seems true of dispositions generally, not just abilities or competences, including the likes of solubility and fragility. Normality, moreover, is not just statistical normality; it is a kind of normality determined implicitly, for any given dispositional concept by those who share that concept.)

Accordingly, there are at least two ways in which your attempt might be unsafe while still apt: first, although not safe *outright*, the attempt might be safe dependently on a circumstantial contingency, awareness of which guides your performance or motivates it rationally; second, although not safe outright, the attempt might be safe dependently on circumstantial normality in various respects, even despite being unguided by any such respects, and rationally motivated by none such.

What is required for aptness is that the performance succeed through the exercise of a competence in a situation appropriately normal for that exercise. A performance that is safe only dependently on a certain contingency, will be apt only if that contingency either guides it or is constitutive of the relevant normalcy of the situation.

The archer's skill is a state that reliably yields accurate shots when applied in normal circumstances. The exercise of the archer's skill is a rational activity in that the archer is guided by reasons. The archer is motivated by reasons to release the arrow when the bow and arrow are held just so. He may be unable to articulate these reasons, but we cannot plausibly require that our reasons must always be articulable, lest we deprive ourselves of reasons that matter to us as much as anything. We identify a loved one, for just one example, in ways that we could not articulate fully. We recognize the loved one on sight based on reasons whose full verbal articulation we cannot plausibly require. Similarly, the archer has reasons for releasing the arrow depending on just how it is then positioned. Of course, if asked to explain why he released it at that point, he could say little beyond "It just felt right to do so." Depending on the target's size and distance, however, it will feel right to release the arrow when positioned in quite different ways. When the archer takes a shot, things relevantly appear quite differently from how they do when he takes another shot. Yet in all such cases it will tend to feel more or less equally right to release the arrow at just the point where the archer does so. However, the specific feeling that qualifies as feeling right will be different from situation to situation, and it is the specific feeling that guides the excellent archer to release the arrow when he does.

The commitments that inform different archers' skill, with respect to various apparent situations, to release the arrow when things appear *thus*, can vary vastly in reliability. The better the archer, the more reliable his commitments; and vice versa.

Some of our relevant commitments come courtesy of Mother Nature and her evolutionary ways, but many others must be learned. The archer's learning requires practice, and seems tantamount to inductive learning. An aspiring archer tries various things, takes note of the degree of resulting success, adjusts accordingly, and with luck remembers what he has learned. What he has learned is not articulable, not fully, but that seems epistemically inessential. He has learned something. When he next takes a shot, he does so based on what he has learned, provided he remembers it well enough.

The same goes for intellectual practice. Much of our intellectual competence comes with our brains, but much is due to learning. The commitments constitutive of learned competences are a varied lot. Some come through explicit instruction, but many come through life experience of enormous scope and variety. Much of our competence, whether practical or intellectual, requires memory. We need to retain it, and it can be lost in various ways, from the localized losses due to lack of practice to the ravages of Alzheimer's.

When a success, practical or intellectual, is creditable to an agent, it is due to an aptitude (to a competence or skill or virtue) seated in that agent, whose exercise is rewarded with success in his act or attitude. Concerning such success, how are we to understand its being *due* to the agent's aptitude? According to one promising proposal, its explanation must saliently involve that aptitude.

We face problems here that mirror problems encountered earlier by the safety proposal. Perhaps, for example, what in the circumstances is explanatorily most salient concerns why the agent retains his competence, or why the situation remains normal. Thus, the evil demon in charge may systematically spoil the competence of agents in an archery competition, or the circumstances of their shots, while making an exception of our successful archer for one of his shots. For that one shot he does not disable the competence or spoil the circumstances. Against that background, what is then explanatorily salient, when we ask why that shot was successful, concerns more the doings of the demon than those of the archer. Despite that, the archer does surely hit his target aptly: his shot is accurate *because* adroit. It seems irrelevant that only luck accounts for his retained competence and propitious circumstances.

Somehow it is the exercise of competence in a normal situation that makes the shot apt: that is, accurate because adroit. That it is apt by luck makes it no less apt.

Let us return, finally, to the value problem for reliabilist conceptions of epistemic justification. The problem is put in proper context only with a distinction between generic reliabilism and virtue epistemology. More specifically, we need to understand that, according to an instrumental conception of justification, a belief is justified by deriving from mechanisms or processes of belief acquisition that reliably deliver true beliefs. True belief seems here installed as a fundamental value of epistemology, while instruments and processes of belief formation are then assessed in respect of how well they deliver that value, and beliefs are granted epistemic status depending on how reliable are the sources from which they derive.[9] This whole way of thinking of epistemology invites the comparison with good coffee and the conundrum as to how true belief could be better for deriving from good sources, if good coffee is no better for deriving from the adroit use of a good coffee maker.

One part at least of the solution to the value problem lies in a point central to virtue epistemology: namely, that the value of apt belief is no less epistemically fundamental

---

[9] I speak of "mechanisms" or processes of belief formation, and sometimes of "input/output mechanisms," but I want to disavow explicitly any implication that these are simple or modular. The process can of course be as subtle and delicate as that of determining whether the butler is guilty, or whether a remark was a deliberate insult, or whether vagueness is epistemic. The epistemic virtues involved need not be as simple as the perception that one seen line is longer than another, though even here there is more than meets the eye, as is shown by the Müller-Lyer illusion. Thus, a mechanism can be something close to a reflex, or it can be a very high-level, central-processing ability of the sort that enables a sensitive critic to "decide" how to assess a work, based on complex and able pondering.

than that of true belief.[10] For this imports a way in which epistemic virtues enter *constitutively* in the attainment of fundamental value, not just instrumentally.[11] Virtues are thus constitutive because the aptness of a belief is constituted by its being accurate because competent. This means that the relevant competences of the agent enter into the constitution of something with fundamental epistemic worth: namely, the apt belief, true because competent.[12]

Our subject has been epistemic normativity, a kind of normative status that a belief attains independently of pragmatic concerns such as those of the athlete or hospital patient. Epistemic normativity is a status by having which a true belief

---

[10] And, perhaps, no more: the true belief, like the accurate shot, is a "success" in its own right. The accurate shot is surely, to that extent, a "successful" shot.

[11] A full account would need to recognize in addition the epistemological value of good omissions, as when one suspends judgment. Cf. Sosa 1991, p. 17.

[12] I am here opting for something like the ballerina's graceful *pas* as correlate of the knower's believing. The apt believing is a performance-immanent value, unlike the cup of coffee vis-à-vis the doings of the barista. Plenty of room remains in the critical domain of epistemology, however, for the kind of value that we find in the work of art that hangs on the museum wall. Take those magnificent works of art, powerful scientific theories. These are often the work of many hands acting collectively. Yet they are obviously important objects of epistemic evaluation. Nor is the only evaluation possible that which is capturable through abstract data-hypothesis relations. The history of science shows how much room there is for further evaluations involving why the theory holds sway in a certain community, including our own, why it is a "live" theory, etc. Some of the relevant factors that explain why it is live, and even held, are only pragmatically relevant, but the abstract observational data/hypothesis relations are unlikely to exhaust those that bear epistemically on the theory's being *properly* (epistemically) live, or *properly* held, etc. Other virtues would seem epistemically pertinent, some of them seated in institutions and not just in individuals distributively. (Developing this point satisfactorily would require distinguishing the theory as a cultural artifact whose "life" depends on how it relates to the community in which it is live from potential theories as just abstract truth bearers. This would be analogous to the distinction between the abstract sequence of propositional contents that constitutes the abstract "play" *Hamlet* throughout eternity, and *Hamlet* as the living cultural artifact, the great play *created* by the genius of Shakespeare.)

constitutes knowledge. We must distinguish the normative status of knowledge as knowledge from the normative status that a bit of knowledge may have by being useful, or deeply explanatory, and so on. Something might be known far better, with greater certainty, and better justification, than something else, while yet the latter knowledge is intellectually finer by far. Compare knowledge that one's back hurts now with some deeply illuminating knowledge about a friend, or a historical period, or a novel, or a scientific theory.

Accordingly, we do well to distinguish between two parts of epistemology: (a) theory of knowledge, and (b) intellectual ethics. The latter concerns evaluation and norms pertinent to intellectual matters generally, with sensitivity to the full span of intellectual values. It is therefore a much broader discipline than a theory of knowledge focused on the nature, conditions, and extent of human knowledge.

That distinction between theory of knowledge and intellectual ethics has drawn a skeptical reaction. Suppose Paul forms a belief about the number of motes of dust on his desk by consulting an Ouija board. According to our proposal, we might then (a) from the point of view of a theory of knowledge, evaluate the belief poorly because the belief is so unsafe with respect to the truth of the matter, and (b) from the point of view of intellectual ethics, criticize the believer for even bothering with such things—from the point of view of his intellectual flourishing, we might say, there are better ways he should be spending his time.

One might be skeptical about this for the following reason:

It seems that we do more than just evaluate the belief negatively from an essentially *performance* point of view when we say that Paul's belief is unjustified. Rather, we subject him to normative criticism for forming a belief this way: we reproach him and find him in some sense blameworthy. Importantly, we do this not *just* because he should have been doing better things with his time, from the point of view of intellectual ethics, but rather because, even with respect to this trivial subject, he has in some sense let us down.

True enough, but the considerations involved in such criticism would still go beyond those involved in the normative status that is *constitutive* of knowledge. The situation seems rather like that of a hunter in a hunting society, in conditions of scarcity, who used energy and resources (arrows) shooting at trivial targets (not live game, say, nor enemies, etc.), and did so carelessly. He would face a loss of credit, and prestige, and might thus forfeit a good position for the next hunt or battle. But this all goes beyond what makes his shot a poor shot. Much later, when the society is agricultural, absent hunting, absent battles, absent even any sport of archery, if someone nevertheless dusts off a bow and some arrows and takes a shot, that shot might be equally poor as a shot, but would incur no such criticism. In an archery-internal sense the shot falls short equally. So, in theory of archery it falls short, and is a "poor" shot. But in respect of the larger ethics of archery, or of the use of bows and arrows, its evaluation would be quite different, and not just in respect of the importance of the targets chosen.

One might be skeptical, moreover, because it is so hard to say much in general about the kinds of questions that are worth pursuing from an intellectual point of view. Thus it is very hard to say why it would be appropriate, from the point of view of intellectual ethics, to criticize someone who spent his time happily learning everything there is to know about some trivial thing (say, the history of bubble gum), while someone who spent their time learning everything there is to know about (say) the us Civil War would escape criticism.

It is worth noting, in response, that one may know that something is so without knowing why it is so. We might know it better if we did know why it was so. But we can know very well that we have a headache even without knowing its cause or explanation. The criticism based on the gum aficionado might indeed just be that he is spending too much time on something too trivial, so that *unless there is some compensating reason*, he can be criticized all things considered. Of course, if he is unable to muster any interest in anything else, and is for whatever reason obsessed with the history of bubble gum, and this is his only way to stave off deep depression, then it's fine. And so on. In any case, recognizing the idea of intellectual ethics, the domain of such evaluations and critical judgments, does not entail any commitment to the idea that it would have to be a domain that we could ever come to understand with a powerful explanatory theory.

Most of the history of epistemology has had the narrower focus of the theory of knowledge. Interest did eventually shift from the focus on the nature of knowledge in the Theaetetus, towards an interest in how far we can be justified in our beliefs generally. But this latter question is that of how extensively we can attain the kind of epistemic justification and aptness that is constitutive of knowledge. It is therefore still a concern in the theory of knowledge, not in intellectual ethics, and so it remains to the present day.

Lecture 5

Virtue, Luck, and Credit

Belief amounts to knowledge when apt: that is to say, when its correctness is attributable to a competence exercised in appropriate conditions. This aptness-centered account was laid out in the second of these lectures, and applied to the problem of dream skepticism. In the third lecture, it helped to explain the nature of intuition and its role in epistemology. In the fourth lecture, it helped to explain epistemic normativity, and to answer a question posed already in Plato's *Meno:* how can knowledge be better than true belief?

The present lecture will aim for a fuller understanding of epistemic competence and of how it secures aptness of belief. Our approach will invoke epistemic sources and their deliverances, on a common understanding rarely made explicit. But first we shall find epistemic competence to be socially as well as individually seated.

A performance is apt if, and only if, it is correct attributably to a competence exercised by the performer, in conditions appropriate for its exercise. By contrast, a performance is safe if, and only if, for some basis that it has, it would not easily have been incorrect if based on that basis. So defined, safety and aptness can come apart. A performance can be apt though unsafe, in at least two ways. The performer's competence might be fragile, for one thing, and its required conditions might be endangered, for another thing. Despite these dangers, the performance might still be apt, however, though of course not safe.

Beliefs are a special case of performances, epistemic performances. When a belief is correct attributably to a competence exercised in its appropriate conditions, it counts as apt and as knowledge of a sort, animal knowledge.

In what follows we tackle two main problems for this account: first the problem of testimony and credit, and then a renewed problem of dreams.

Testimony is among our most important sources of knowledge. Most of what we know about the world beyond the scope of our personal experience is owed to the say-so, oral or written, of our fellow human beings. Each of us is blessed with that source, constituted by a disposition to receive others' say-so when we hear it or read it. And this poses a problem for the view of animal knowledge as apt belief.

Any belief that is knowledge must be correct, but must it be correct due to an epistemic competence? That seems strained at best for knowledge derived from testimony. That it derives from testimony does little to explain the correctness of a belief so derived. Others no doubt made the relevant discovery—perhaps a historian, or a detective, or a scientist, or a physician—and the information was then passed down, resulting in some later recipient's belief, whose correctness then owes little to his own individual accomplishment, if all he does is to receive the information.

If the correctness of that eventual belief is attributable to a competence, it is not one seated in the believer individually. Any such competence would have to be socially seated instead, in some broader social unit. But there seems no organized social entity to whose competence we can attribute that correctness. A competence might be socially seated, however, without being seated in a social organization. Consider a group of passers-by, each a stranger to the others, who spot someone crushed by a fallen tree, and leap in unison to lift the tree off the victim. A competence seated in them collectively is manifest in the performance of the good deed, a highly complex act to which they all contribute.

Compare those who join together across time in the exercise of a competence manifest eventually in a belief received through testimony. These form no organization, no socially organized entity. Yet their joint effort eventuates in the correctness of the present belief. Consider the individual competences that join together to form the collective social competence resulting in the correctness of that final belief. These will include this believer's own competence to trust testimony, which helps account, at least in some small part, for why his belief is correct.

Something similar holds good of socially seated competence generally. A quarterback may throw a touchdown pass, for example, thus exercising a competence. But this individual competence is only one part of a broader competence, seated in the whole offensive team, that more fully explains the successful touchdown pass, the apt performance of that quarterback. The pass receiver's competence may be crucial, for example, along with the individual competences of the offensive linesmen, and so on.

If we think of animal knowledge as apt belief, and of belief as apt when correct attributably to a competence, then the fullest credit often belongs to a group, even a motley group. Seated in the group collectively is a competence whose complex exercise leads through testimonial links to the correctness of one's present belief. The correctness of one's belief is still attributable in part to a competence seated in oneself individually, but the credit that one earns will then be partial at best. The quarterback's pass derives from his competence, but its great success, its being a *touchdown* pass manifests more fully the team's competence. Similarly for one's testimony-derived belief.

It may be replied that partial credit cannot be sufficient for knowledge, as is shown by Gettier counterexamples. We have concluded that a belief will count as apt if correct attributably to an individual competence, amounting thus to animal knowledge. Objection: a Gettier victim would then be said to know through his justified true belief. Suppose you conclude that someone here owns a Ford, for example, by first amassing evidence that Nogot does, and then drawing a simple existential conclusion. If aptness requires only partial credit, you then seem to know that someone here owns a Ford, since your true belief seems partially attributable to an epistemic competence seated in you. But you fail to know nonetheless, if you infer that someone here owns a Ford from your false belief that Nogot does, when only Havit does.

Something may explain the existence of a certain entity, however, without even partially explaining why it has a given property. That it was made in a Volvo factory may explain the existence of a certain defective car, for example, without even partially explaining why it is now defective. Indeed it may be defective *despite* being a Volvo. Its being defective is hence not at all attributable to its origin in that Volvo factory.

Similarly, the true belief that someone here owns a Ford may owe its existence to an exercise of some epistemic

competence without owing its correctness to that competence. The Gettier subject concludes that someone owns a
Ford based on his belief that Nogot does, and this reasoning
helps explain the existence of his belief in that true conclusion. Since Nogot owns no Ford, however, the reasoning
via Nogot fails to explain how the believer gets it right in
concluding that someone here owns a Ford. The reasoning
by way of Nogot does of course help explain why the believer
has that belief, but it does not in the slightest help explain its
correctness. In order to do so, it would have to be a factor that,
either singly or in combination with other factors, accounts
for how the belief is true rather than false. This means that it
must help establish a connection between how the believer
believes on that matter, and the truth of the matter. But the
belief about Nogot helps establish no such connection with
the truth of the matter at hand: whether someone here owns
a Ford.[1]

It might be argued that there being my true belief that
someone here owns a Ford is explained by the combination
of there being the belief at all with that content, and the
truth of the content. So, for the explanation of the whole
explanandum you need the part of the explanation that
accounts for why the belief is there at all with that content.
And this will require adverting to the belief that Nogot owns
a Ford. The error resides however, in supposing that what

---

[1] Our account does help to bring out, however, how not all Gettier cases
are created equal. In some cases, such as Gettier's two actual examples, and such
as Lehrer's Nogot/Havit case, the subject does not attain so much as animal
knowledge: apt belief, belief that gets it right in a way sufficiently attributable to
the exercise of a competence in its proper conditions. However, in other similar
cases what the subject lacks is rather reflective knowledge. Our kaleidoscope
perceiver, in Lecture 2, is a case in point. The Ginet/Goldman barns example
arguably belongs with the kaleidoscope case.

explains there being my true belief is what explains why my belief is true. It is helpful here to compare the fact that what explains why there is this defective car in existence may not even partially explain why this car is defective. Thus its having come forth from a Volvo factory may be part of the explanation for why there is this defective car in existence, and indeed for why there is something in existence that is both a car and defective. But its having come forth from a Volvo factory still may not in the slightest explain why this car is defective, if the defect derives, for example, from some later sequence of states or events, such as those constitutive of improper maintenance.

Partial credit might hence suffice for aptness, and so for animal knowledge, without risk of Gettier refutation. The Gettier victim's belief is owed in part to his exercise of an epistemic competence without the *correctness* of that belief being similarly owed. Testimonial knowledge can therefore take the form of a belief whose correctness is attributable to a complex social competence only partially seated in that individual believer. The account of animal knowledge as apt, creditable belief can thus explain how testimony-derived knowledge might count as apt, creditable belief, despite how little of the credit for the belief's correctness may belong to the believer individually.[2]

---

[2] Again, aptness is a matter of degree even beyond the degrees imported by its constitutive adroitness and accuracy, for a performance is apt only if its success is *sufficiently* attributable to the performer's competence. This leads to the awkward result that one of two performances can be more apt than the other, without either one being apt. Compare such threshold-dependent categories as that of being tall, large, heavy, etc. These are all cases in which x can be more F than y without either x or y being F. So a success can be more creditable to x than to y without being creditable to either. Neither would earn so much as partial credit, then, for their performance.

Next we return to the problem of dreams, of how our perceptual beliefs can ever amount to animal knowledge given that we might just be dreaming a dream that includes beliefs based on sensory experience just like the experience constitutive of wakeful perception.

Safety is preferable to sensitivity as a requirement for knowledge. For one thing, it is in line with our common sense presupposition that we are not currently envatted, nor even just misled. If one were misled, one's belief that one was not misled would remain, on the same basis. That simple belief hence fails the test of sensitivity. But it passes the test of safety, which requires only that not easily would it be held yet false. However, even the safety of perceptual beliefs is put in doubt by the proximity of the dream scenario. If while dreaming we hold beliefs based on sensory experiences like those of waking life, then any perceptual beliefs might too easily have been false though held on the same sensory basis, while dreaming. That is why knowledge requires not safety but aptness. Our perceptual beliefs are apt, despite how easily we might have been dreaming, so long as they are correct attributably to the exercise of a perceptual competence in its appropriate conditions. Animal knowledge is thus apt belief.

That account seems refuted, however, by the jokester who controls both the ambient light and the color of a kaleidoscope surface seen by a nearby perceiver. So situated he cannot know the surface to be red, despite believing it to be red through his color vision exercised in its appropriate conditions. Does this refute the account of knowledge as apt belief? No, we can defend the account by distinguishing two sorts of knowledge. The perceiver can lack knowledge of one sort, namely reflective knowledge, or apt belief aptly noted (or presupposed, taken for granted, etc.), while retaining knowledge of another sort: animal knowledge, or apt belief *simpliciter.*

Human knowledge is what we wish to understand, the ordinary knowledge of human beings. The skeptic alleges common sense to be incompatible with our knowing the external world through perception, the past through memory, our neighbors through their behavior, and so on. In wielding his radical scenarios, however, the skeptic foists on common sense a requirement of absolute safety. Common sense makes no such requirement; it requires absolute safety for *absolute* knowledge, perhaps, but not for ordinary knowledge. Reasonable safety is enough for ordinary knowledge. That is why the problem of dreams is more interesting than the problem of envatment. Ordinary human knowledge requires only reasonable safety, not a failsafe guarantee. Even so, the problem of dreams is still with us, since the dream scenario is too close for comfort, given how naturally and often we dream. Can we perhaps solve the problem by dispensing with safety altogether, and requiring aptness instead?

If the real possibility that the light is bad deprives the kaleidoscope perceiver of knowledge, then the real possibility that we dream deprives us of ordinary perceptual knowledge. Defeating the dream skeptic therefore requires defending the kaleidoscope perceiver. Although he lacks knowledge of a sort, *reflective* knowledge, the kaleidoscope perceiver retains a more basic sort of knowledge, animal knowledge. Is this a satisfyingly stable position?

The kaleidoscope perceiver does seem to exercise his competent color vision in its appropriate conditions. These include his open-eyed alertness, the well-lit medium, the proximity and size of the unoccluded surface, etc. Plausibly, he gets it right, in believing the seen surface to be red, through the exercise of a perceptual competence in its appropriate conditions. Yet the jokester could as easily give him a bad combination (red-light+white-surface) as the good actual combination (white-light+red-surface). The knowledge he is thus denied is only *reflective* knowledge, however, while he still knows in the more basic, animal way. His object-level belief is correct attributably to his object-level visual competence.

Analogously, the perceptual knowledge that dreams threaten to preclude is at the *reflective* and not at the animal level. Accordingly, the relation of the kaleidoscope perceiver to the bad light possibility must be distinguished from the relation of the ordinary perceiver to the equally proximate dream possibility. These must be distinguished in such a way that the ordinary perceiver can know not only at the animal level but also at the reflective level through his ordinary perceptual beliefs, even while the kaleidoscope perceiver falls short. That the kaleidoscope perceiver falls short epistemically *in some important way* is so plausible intuitively that it must be given its due. I say the kaleidoscope perceiver falls short of reflective knowledge: he fails to know that he knows. This means that in believing his object belief to be apt he fails to believe aptly. But why, exactly, does his meta-belief fail to be apt, why is it not itself correct attributably to any meta-competence?

My earlier lecture gave only a sketchy answer to this question. What follows will attempt to do more. What, to begin with, *are* the competences potentially involved: the object-level competence, and the meta-level competence? What indeed is an epistemic competence in general?

One interesting answer invokes a traditional conception of epistemic sources and their deliverances.

Traditionally our knowledge is said to have "sources" such as perception, memory, and inference. Epistemic sources issue "deliverances" that we may or may not accept. Our senses may issue the deliverance about two adjacent lines that one is longer, for example, a deliverance rejected by those in the know about the Müller-Lyer illusion.

A deliverance of <p> to a subject S is a "saying" that p, one witnessed by S. Different sources involve different ways of saying that p. Someone may say it literally, of course, in person or in writing, and S may hear it or read it. If we can believe our eyes or ears, moreover, it's because they tell us things. We experience visually or aurally as if p. Normally we accept the deliverances of our senses, unless we detect something untoward.

Deliverances thus conceived make up a realm of the ostensible: ostensible perceptions, ostensible memories, ostensible conclusions, ostensible intuitions, and the like. We may or may not believe our eyes or ears, we may or may not trust our senses, or our memory, or our calculations or other reasonings.

Take any deliverance, by which I mean here *any particular delivering of a certain propositional content.* Any such deliverance is safe *outright* provided it would then so deliver its content only if true. A deliverance is safe *dependently* on some further fact if, and only if, though not safe outright, it would still so deliver its content, *in the presence of that further fact,* only if true.

Most often, when one accepts the deliverances of one's senses at face value, one does so in appropriate conditions for doing so, and such deliverances are then safe outright, because nothing threatens the appropriateness of the conditions. Given the jokester in the wings, however, the deliverance of the kaleidoscope perceiver's color vision is no longer safe outright. In order to constitute animal knowledge that the surface is red, the perceiver's belief must then apparently be based not only on that color deliverance, but also on the quality of the light.[3]

Put yourself in the place of the kaleidoscope perceiver. Given the jokester, that you see a red surface is something you can know only if you base your belief on the reason that the light is good. However, a belief based essentially on a basis can amount to knowledge only if the believer knows the basis to be true.[4] But the jokester precludes your knowing the light to be good. How then can you know the seen surface to be red? We need a closer look at deliverances and at how accepting a deliverance can give us knowledge.

---

[3] *Outright* safety is not a requirement for knowledge, in any case, since a belief might amount to knowledge if guided by a condition dependently on which it is safe, even though one might easily enough have so believed based only on some other condition, dependently on which one's belief would not have been safe. Thus, one may have a good look and trust one's eyes in believing that p, and thus come to know that p, even if one might then too easily have trusted a lying bystander instead. So, one's belief is not safe outright, since it might too easily have been false. The more plausible requirement is *dependent* safety, safety dependent on a fact that also guides one's belief. That the bells toll might be something one knows by trusting the deliverances of one's good eyesight in its appropriate conditions, even if one might easily have trusted instead one's unreliable hearing, despite too much noise, misleading loudspeakers, etc. So, one's belief that the bells toll is not then safe outright, but it is safe as a belief based on the deliverance of one's sense of sight.

[4] Here I am relying on two senses of "basing." Someone might base a belief that p on a "factual" reason, say the fact that q, by virtue of basing that belief on his awareness that q, where this awareness might take the form of a belief or perhaps the form of a propositional experience. If we are thus liberal on the ways a factual reason can form a basis, then we need to be similarly liberal about the form of knowledge required, which can now be highly implicit, and need not be linguistically expressible by the subject.

Examples of deliverances are test results, indicator readings, eyewitness reports, media reports, perceptual appearances, and even rational intuitions and ostensible conclusions.[5] Contents are delivered by each such source. Acceptance of a deliverance thereby constitutes knowledge only if the source is reliable, and operates in its appropriate conditions, so that the deliverance is safe, while the correctness of one's acceptance is attributable to one's epistemic competence.[6]

---

[5] Here and in what follows I no longer distinguish explicitly in every case between deliverances as deliverings and deliverances as items delivered. I will rely on context to disambiguate.

[6] One might of course know something through accepting a deliverance that is safe only dependently on a certain condition, so long as one accepts the deliverance based not only on its being a deliverance of its sort, but also on the holding of the condition. Thus, the deliverances of a speedometer that works sporadically might still be safe relative to the needle's being unstuck. Someone can know by accepting those deliverances guided by this condition, even if one who accepts them without such guidance would not share that knowledge. The difference is that the speedometer is then safe concerning the speed *dependently* on its needle's being unstuck.

Knowledge that a bird is flying by can be accidental by deriving from a casual glance in the right direction at the right time. The correct belief about the bird's flight is accidental, then, but in a way that contrasts with the belief of a driver who reads a speedometer that happens to be stuck on the right speed. In both cases the subject accepts a deliverance as such, but only the bird watcher accepts a safe deliverance. Not so the driver, whose readings are safe only dependently on a condition, the needle's not being stuck, by which she then fails to be guided.

It would not be enough to require that source X's deliverances merely guide S to believe the contents thus delivered. It must be required rather that X's deliverances guide S to accept those deliverances *as such*. S must accept the contents thus delivered as such, and this accepting must be guided by the deliverances, i.e., by the deliverings (and guided also by the factors dependently on which those deliverances are safe). Reason: what the absence of the deliverance would properly take away is its content's being accepted for the reason that it is thus delivered, on the basis of the deliverance; after all, that content might *also* be a deliverance of some other source, in which case it would not and should not be renounced merely because the first deliverance is rejected.

As for the notion of "guiding," let us understand this as nothing more than the converse of "basing": Factor F "guides" belief B if and only if belief B is "based" on F (perhaps in combination with other factors).

Deliverances are "indications" when safe. A deliverance/indication I(p) "indicates" outright that p if, and only if, I(p) would be delivered only if it were so that p; and it indicates that p "dependently on condition C" if, and only if, both C obtains and C would obtain while I(p) was delivered only if it were so that p (although it is false that I(p) would be delivered only if it were so that p).

What then is required for someone to attain animal knowledge based on an indication? Here is one idea:

(I) S has animal knowledge that p based on indication I(p) only if either (a) I(p) indicates the truth outright and S accepts that indication as such outright, or (b) for some condition C, I(p) indicates the truth dependently on C and S accepts that indication as such, not outright, but guided by C (so that S accepts the indication as such *on the basis* of C).

Unfortunately, condition (I) will give the bad result that the kaleidoscope perceiver lacks animal knowledge. This at least is what we must say if we accept the following condition:

(F) S knows that p guided essentially by the fact that q (or based on the reason that q, or based on the fact that q), only if S knows that q.

Given F, the kaleidoscope perceiver does not know the seen surface to be red, if he can know it only guided by the fact that the light is good. The jokester precludes his knowing the light to be good.

What is thus true of the kaleidoscope case, because too easily might the light be bad, would then seem true of perceptual beliefs in general, because too easily might one be dreaming. So, we would be deprived of our solution to the problem of dreams.

In order to retrieve that solution, we modify our indication condition:

(I′) S has animal knowledge that p based on indication I(p) only if either (a) I(p) indicates the truth outright and S accepts that indication as such outright, or (b) for some condition C, I(p) indicates the truth dependently on C and either (i) S accepts that indication as such not outright but guided by C (so that S accepts the indication as such on the basis of C), *or else (ii) C is constitutive of the appropriate normalcy of the conditions for the competence exercised by S in accepting I(p).*[7]

That the light is good is constitutive of the appropriate normalcy of the conditions for the competence exercised by the kaleidoscope perceiver. Accordingly, it is not required by (I′) that the perceiver know that the light is good. Nor is it required by (I′) that the ordinary perceiver know that he is awake. Both the kaleidoscope perceiver and the ordinary perceiver can retain their animal perceptual knowledge even without knowing that the conditions are appropriately normal for the exercise of their perceptual competences. Nevertheless, the kaleidoscope perceiver and the ordinary perceiver are still dramatically different epistemically. They differ in whether they can know their respective conditions to be appropriately normal for the exercise of their perceptual

---

[7] Again, condition b(ii) might better require that C be constitutive of conditions that are appropriately normal or *better* for the operation of that source. (Note that even when the conditions are better, what matters is that they be conditions *for the operation of that source.* Such conditions would not be ones that would deliver the good deliverance on their own, without the source being operative.

competence. The jokester precludes the kaleidoscope perceiver from knowing this; but, despite how easily he might
be dreaming, the ordinary perceiver is not similarly affected.
Or so I will argue.

Some epistemic competences are dispositions to host a distinctive range of deliverances in certain coordinated circumstances. These deliverances are intellectual seemings, whereby
the subject is attracted to assent to the content delivered.
Other epistemic competences are dispositions to accept such
deliverances at face value, absent any sign to the contrary.

The first of our two sorts of epistemic dispositions are
"epistemic sources." A source is thus a disposition to receive
a certain range of deliverances in certain conditions. Our
second sort of epistemic competence is a disposition implicitly
to trust a source. Think of the deliverances of the senses,
or testimony, or memory, or reasoning, and so on. Some
epistemic competences are dispositions to trust such a source
absent any special sign to the contrary. Of course, sources are
trustworthy only in conditions appropriate for their operation.

Such a disposition can be a "competence" only if its contained source is sufficiently reliable, at least in its distinctively
appropriate conditions. So our color vision, as an epistemic
competence, would involve a disposition to accept that a
seen surface has a certain color if it appears to have that color,
absent any sign to the contrary.[8]

Someone with good color vision has a distinctive cluster
of dispositions to accept propositional contents, among them

---

[8] Consider one's sources, one's dispositions to receive deliverances in certain
distinctive ranges, i.e., one's dispositions to have corresponding intellectual
seemings. Such a source, if reliable, will itself constitute a kind of "epistemic
competence," in a broader sense.)

the following: to take it that one sees a red surface when one seems to see a red surface. A perceptual epistemic competence is thus constituted by a disposition implicitly to accept a range of material conditionals of the following form: if it appears F, then it is F. Each competence will have a distinctive range of such conditionals, and distinctive appropriate conditions. Thus, color vision will concern color properties, and the appropriate conditions will concern quality of light, distance, occlusion, size, and so on. These would be conditions to which we humans implicitly relativize in our wish to know of one's own and one's peers' abilities to tell what's what in the relevant range; and conditions to which we implicitly relativize in trusting such abilities.

What the kaleidoscope perceiver presupposes is not the strong conditional that the surface would not appear red were it not red (a falsehood), or that the surface would appear red only if really red (also false), but only the material conditional that if the surface appears red then it is red (a truth). That is what we must say in order to defend his animal knowledge, and by extension the animal knowledge of the ordinary perceiver. For if what one must presuppose in trusting the deliverances of our senses is the stronger conditional, then neither the kaleidoscope perceiver nor the ordinary perceiver will attain so much as animal knowledge. Neither the strong conditionals of the kaleidoscope perceiver nor the strong conditionals of the ordinary perceiver will be true. Too easily in each case might the deliverance have been delivered while false, in one case because the light might so easily have been bad, in the other case because the subject might so easily have been dreaming.

More is of course required for animal knowledge than simply that the implicit material conditional be true. When

such a conditional functions as a rational basis for a perceiver's belief, this belief can amount to knowledge only if the
basis belief (or presupposition) is knowledge as well. The basis
belief must therefore be apt, which means that its correctness
must be due to the exercise of a competence. What competence might it exercise? Answer: just the default competence
that is manifest through one's implicit, dispositional acceptance of that range of material conditionals as one approaches
any new situation ready to perceive. When that competence
is exercised in its normal conditions it yields truth, at least
predominantly. And, in any particular instance, the exercise
of that competence *in its normal conditions* would yield truth.
This remains so even when there is a jokester in the wings.

We have defended the kaleidoscope perceiver's animal
knowledge because that is crucial to our defense of our
ordinary perceptual knowledge from dream skepticism, given
their relevant parity. However, we must also find some
difference between the two, since it is intuitively so plausible
that in some more demanding way the kaleidoscope perceiver
would not know, whereas ordinary perceivers routinely do
still know in that way.

Reflective knowledge goes beyond animal knowledge,
and requires also an apt apprehension that the object-level
perceptual belief is apt. What competence might a believer
exercise in gaining such meta-apprehension? It would have to
be a competence enabling him to size up the appropriateness
of the conditions. Absent special reason for caution, the
kaleidoscope perceiver exercises a default competence, by
presuming the conditions to be appropriate, in taking his
visual appearance at face value. Moreover, it is by hypothesis
true that the conditions are appropriate. So, the kaleidoscope
perceiver is right about the conditions, and he is even right

that he believes aptly that the seen surface is red. But that is not enough. His meta-apprehension will be apt and thus knowledge only if its *correctness* is attributable to a meta-competence. Is this further requirement met?

Recall our principle C:

C. For any correct belief (or presupposition) that p, its correctness is attributable to a competence only if it derives from the exercise of that competence in conditions appropriate for its exercise, where that exercise in those conditions would not too easily have issued a false belief (or presupposition).

If the kaleidoscope perceiver's meta-competence is to yield knowledge, therefore, it must *not* be excessively liable to yield a falsehood when exercised in its appropriate conditions. Given the jokester, however, this requirement is not met, since too easily then might the perceiver have been misled in trusting the conditions to be appropriate in that default way.

The kaleidoscope perceiver has animal knowledge but lacks reflective knowledge. He has apt belief *simpliciter*, but lacks apt belief aptly presumed apt. This is in line with our intuition that somehow he falls short. The knowledge that he lacks, given the jokester, is reflective knowledge.

What of our ordinary perceptual knowledge, given the dream scenario? Can our perceptual beliefs reach the reflective level? They do reach the animal level, for they remain true attributably to our perceptual competences exercised in appropriate conditions, despite the proximate dream scenario. However, does not the ordinary perceiver join the kaleidoscope perceiver in failing aptly to apprehend the aptness of his

object-level beliefs? If so, the skeptic wins: ordinary perceptual knowledge then falls short of the reflective level. In our
most ordinary perceptual beliefs we would be in the position
of the kaleidoscope perceiver. So we would fall short epistemically, massively so, just as the skeptic has always alleged.

Fortunately, the cases are disanalogous. Even on the orthodox conception, dreams may differ substantially in content
from the normal content of wakeful perception. In addition, when asleep and dreaming we could hardly use the
same epistemic competences as in wakeful perception, in
their appropriate conditions. The very fact that we are asleep
and dreaming destroys the appropriate normalcy of such
conditions. Moreover, when asleep and dreaming we are
unlikely to retain our normal competence for sizing up our
object-level beliefs and competences.

Compare the kaleidoscope perceiver, threatened by the
jokester, with the ordinary perceiver, threatened by the
dream scenario. The object-level competence of the kaleidoscope perceiver is exercised in its appropriately normal
conditions, despite the fact that both the competence and
the conditions are endangered by the jokester. The object-
level competence of the ordinary perceiver, too, is exercised
in its appropriate conditions, even if the dream scenario
endangers both his competence and its required conditions.
Both the kaleidoscope perceiver and the ordinary perceiver
therefore enjoy perceptual apt belief and animal knowledge.
However, the bad-light possibility deprives the kaleidoscope
perceiver of reflective knowledge, while the dream possibility does not analogously deprive the ordinary perceiver of
reflective knowledge. Why so?

First, the kaleidoscope perceiver does not *aptly* pre-
sume his object-level perceptual belief to be apt. Any

meta-competence in view through which he might get it right in so presuming, seems one that either: (a) is exercised in its normal, minimal conditions ("no apparent sign to the contrary"), but might too easily have been exercised to the effect of a false presumption, given the jokester; or else (b) is not exercised in its normal conditions, since the very presence of the jokester already spoils the conditions.

By contrast, the ordinary believer can aptly apprehend the aptness of his object-level perceptual belief. For, he can get it right in so presuming through a meta-competence exercised in its appropriate normal conditions. The relevant meta-competence is a default competence of taking it for granted that conditions are appropriately normal, absent some specific sign to the contrary. When asleep and dreaming we exercise no such competence, since:

(i)   in a dream there *would* be signs to the contrary (recall Austin and Descartes), unlike how it is for the misled kaleidoscope perceiver;

and since:

(ii)   when asleep we would not be using unimpaired the same relevant faculties that we use when we perceive our environment while awake.

The position of the ordinary perceiver vis-à-vis the dream scenario is thus different from that of the kaleidoscope perceiver vis-à-vis the jokester scenario. We can hence insist, against the dream skeptic, that in ordinary perception we acquire both perceptual apt belief, or animal knowledge, and perceptual apt belief aptly presumed apt, or reflective knowledge.

We now have a way to defend our ordinary perceptual knowledge as reflective and not only animal. Our virtue-based way is applicable both against the dream scenario and against the more radical "hallucination" scenarios. We thus go beyond our earlier defense based on the imagination model. That defense protects our perceptual knowledge at the animal level, and underwrites perceptual knowledge as reflective, but does this only against the dream scenario. We wish of course to protect our ordinary knowledge as reflective not only from the dream scenarios but also from the more radical scenarios. And it is this more ambitious defense that requires us to go beyond the imagination model, to our later virtue-theoretic reflections.

However, it may still be thought that any such more ambitious defense must fall into vicious circularity. The sixth, concluding, lecture will take up this hoary objection. Its topic is the traditional Pyrrhonian Problematic, "The Problem of the Criterion," that of how we could possibly attain reflective knowledge, apt belief that we aptly believe, through any of the traditional sources of knowledge, either singly or in combination.

Lecture 6

The Problem of the Criterion

Three leading ideas will guide us, each independently plausible, and all in line with the virtue epistemology defended in earlier lectures.

First, knowledge is a matter of degree, in various respects. Holmes and Watson may both know something, while Holmes knows it better. Among the things that Holmes knows, moreover, some he knows better than others. This comports with our conception of animal knowledge as apt belief, since aptness of belief admits degrees in three respects: in respect of the competence exercised, in respect of the quality of the conditions, and in respect of how much the correctness of the belief is due to that competence exercised in those conditions. There is also a higher level of knowledge—reflective knowledge, apt belief aptly noted—which imports further gradations.

Prominent among things we hold dear, according to a *second* leading idea, is the coherence of our minds. When constituted by inter-belief explanatory relations, such coherence goes with the value of understanding. We want our beliefs to be so integrated as to enable answers for our many and varied whys.

A *third* idea will also figure eventually: namely, that the evaluation of a particular entity, such as an action or a belief, can be importantly relational. In a landscape, or a poem, or a conversation, at a certain point something may fit well or ill, and if the former, it is then relevantly "appropriate," or perhaps even "required." The object of evaluation is thus a particular item, but it is evaluated relative to its relevant wider context. And the wider context of evaluation may include possibility space, as when an archer hits the bull's-eye with a shot that is not only accurate but also "skillful," with its counterfactual implications. A belief may similarly hit the mark of truth unaided by luck, and may also fit within the believer's wider body of beliefs. And we can then evaluate it as "epistemically justified," in one or another sense: "competently adroit" perhaps (or reliably based, or counterfactually safe, etc.), or perhaps "rationally justified" (coherently fitting, and held in part on that basis).

Guided by these three ideas, we next consider two seemingly trivial principles, which together hold surprising consequences. Drawing and assessing these will be our main project.

A. Some consequences of two principles

First the principles:

Ascent (principle of epistemic ascent).
If one knows full well that p and considers whether one knows that p, *then* one must be justified in thinking that one does.[1]

---

[1] The locution "is justified in thinking that p" thus stands for "is justified in (actually) thinking that p" and not just for "would be justified in thinking that p." Knowing being a matter of degree, to know full well is to know in such a way that one's belief lies above some threshold(s) along some dimension(s) inherently

Closure (principle of the closure of epistemic justification through justifiedly believed entailment).

If one is fully justified in believing p and in believing that, necessarily, unless it is so that q, it cannot be so that p, *then* one must also be justified in believing that q.

These principles both concern the conscious contents of a mind at a given time. Ascent, for example, when spelled out more fully, reads thus:

If, at a given time when one knows full well that p, one consciously considers whether one knows that p, *then* one must also be justified in affirming that one does.

Why should we believe this? Anything one knows full well must be something of which one is sufficiently confident. Suppose that, while consciously confident that p, one also considers, at that same time, whether one not only believes but knows that p. Exactly three options open up: one might say either (a) "No, I don't know that," or (b) "Who knows whether I know it or not; maybe I do, maybe I don't," or (c) "Yes, that is something I do know." One is better off, surely, if able to give the later answers: better off with the second answer than with the first, and better off yet with the third. Answer (a), and even answer (b), would reveal a certain lack of integration in that stretch of consciousness; only answer (c), of the three, entirely avoids disharmony within that consciousness at that time. If one has to give answer (a), or even answer (b), one thereby falls short, and one's belief that p itself falls short. That belief is then not all that it could be. One is not as well

---

involved in a belief's status as a piece of knowledge. On our virtue epistemology that would be some dimension inherently involved in the status of the belief as apt, or as aptly presumed apt.

justified as one might be, epistemically. You are best justified in consciously believing that p at that time if you can answer in the affirmative your own conscious question whether in so believing you thereby know. You are better justified in so believing if able to answer thus affirmatively than if consciously forced to withhold judgment; and you are especially better justified in so believing if able to answer thus affirmatively than if consciously led to *deny* that you know.[2]

---

[2] Talk of "justification" among epistemologists varies in its reference and probably in its meaning. Some might reject our idea that one *is* better *justified* epistemically in believing that p if one can see oneself as justified, and that one's belief, one's believing, is itself thereby better justified (in some relational way, as suggested in n. 1). If so, I am inclined not so much to debate them as to switch terminology. Thus I might say that one is then "better off" epistemically in having that belief, or that one's belief is more reasonable or has a higher epistemic status since more defensible rationally, or the like. The important points are these: first, knowing full well is knowing that attains some desirably high level of epistemic quality; second, defensibility in the arena of reflection is a relevant dimension of such epistemic quality, especially when underwritten by *apt* belief that the core belief is apt; third, we can understand traditional skepticism as concerned largely with the circularity that seems eventually required if one is to satisfy the demands of such reflective knowledge. So, when the skeptic denies that we know, he is often, and most deeply, best interpreted as denying that we know thus *reflectively*. Finally, it will be superficial to reply to *this* skeptic by saying, in effect, that *animal* knowledge requires no such reflective status, and that ordinarily we most often rest content with claims to and possession of such animal knowledge. So, the skeptic's circularity concerns simply don't bear on the attainability of the sort of knowledge that normally concerns us. This response is superficial, and does not deepen much even if it turns out that there is no different *sense* or *meaning* of the word "knowledge" in English that corresponds to *reflective* knowledge. Suppose there is a *state* of reflective knowledge as understood here, and suppose we see it to be an epistemically desirable state, above that of belief that is otherwise the same but stays at the mere animal level. So long as all of that is the case, skepticism about *reflective* knowledge will retain its traditional interest. In addition, as a separate point, there are the advantages claimed for recognition of a kind of knowledge, reflective knowledge, above the animal level, enabling appeal to this in understanding some of the skeptical dialectic even when restricted to skepticism about animal knowledge. For, as argued earlier, it may be that some of the supposed intuitions that would deny us

Suppose the knowledge at issue in the antecedent of Ascent to be knowledge of our coherence-requiring high quality. A belief would not qualify as a case of such knowledge if enmeshed in a debilitating incoherence—as when one has to accompany one's belief, at that same time, with a conscious denial that it is knowledge, or even with a conscious suspension of judgment. If it is knowledge of that high level that is involved in our principle, then the combination of the two conjuncts in its antecedent requires the truth of its consequent. One does not attain high-level knowledge, when one consciously wonders whether one does know, unless one is able to say yes. What is more, to say yes arbitrarily would not do. One's belief amounts to reflective knowledge only if one can say that one does know, not just arbitrarily, but with adequate justification.

Our principle of Closure, too, concerns the fully conscious contents of a mind at a given time, so that, when spelled out more fully, it reads like this:

> *If*, at a given time, one *consciously* believes both that p, and that, necessarily, unless it is so that q it cannot be so that p, *then* one is fully justified in these two beliefs only if one is also justified in then *affirming that q*. '

Suppose, again, one consciously believes that p, and, at that same time, second, one consciously believes that, by logical necessity, if p then q. Exactly three options open up on the

knowledge *tout court* in certain hypothetical cases are best interpreted as intuitions to the effect that we lack *reflective* knowledge rather than just animal knowledge. Having the concept of reflective knowledge readily available, whether or not we think that the English word "knowledge" is ambiguous, will enable us to accommodate certain intuitions that otherwise would prove problematic to our account of *animal* knowledge. This form of argument was used above, especially in Lecture 5.

proposition that q: either (a) one might deny it, assenting consciously to its very negation, or (b) one might consciously withhold judgment on it, thinking consciously: who knows, maybe it's true, maybe it's false, or (c) one might consciously affirm it. One is better off, surely, if able to give the later answers: better off with the second answer than with the first, and better off yet with the third. Answer (a), and even answer (b), would reveal a certain lack of integration; only answer (c), of the three, avoids disharmony. If one has to give answer (a), or even answer (b), one falls short, and either one's belief that p or one's belief that, necessarily, if p then q, itself falls short. At least one of these beliefs is then not all that it could be. One is not as well justified as one might be, epistemically, in that belief. One is best justified in consciously believing both that p and that, necessarily, if p then q, at that time, only if one can also assent consciously to the proposition that q. One is better justified in so believing, anyhow, if one can thus consciously affirm that q, than if one has to suspend judgment on it, or, worse, consciously *deny* it.

Suppose the justification at issue in the antecedent of Closure is justification of our coherence-requiring high quality, so that incoherent beliefs would not be thus justified—as when one believes that p and that, necessarily, if p then q, and yet consciously denies that q, or consciously suspends judgment. If so, if it is justification of that coherence-requiring level that is involved in our principle, then the combination of the two conjuncts in its antecedent requires the truth of its consequent. One does not attain the epistemic heights required for high-level conscious justification—both that p and that, necessarily, if p then q—unless one also consciously assents to the proposition that q; and one must assent not just arbitrarily but with adequate justification.[3]

From these two principles—Ascent and Closure—we may already derive a principle with a substantial role in recent and not-so-recent epistemology:

Exclusion (principle of exclusion).
If one knows full well that p and considers whether one knows that p, *and* one is then fully justified in believing that, necessarily, unless it is so that q one cannot know that p, *then* one must also be justified in believing that q.

This follows straightforwardly. Via Ascent, the first two conjuncts of the antecedent of Exclusion entail this: that one is justified in believing that one knows that p. And this, in combination with the third conjunct, via Closure in turn yields: that one is justified in believing that q. Putting all this together, we see Exclusion entailed by Ascent and Closure. Of course, our focus is still a single time when someone consciously believes and considers the relevant items. So the knowing, considering, and justified believing that Exclusion concerns is all to take place in a single consciousness at the same time.

Exclusion implies that if one is to know full well that p while consciously believing it, then if one also consciously considers whether one knows that p, while consciously believing with full justification that unless q one cannot possibly know that p, then one must justifiedly believe that q.

---

[3] Here I assume that anyone who consciously assents to the propositions that p and that, necessarily, if p then q, must occupy one of exactly three positions on the question whether q: assenting, dissenting, consciously suspending judgment. If this assumption is incorrect, however, that would require only a minor revision to our principle—namely, specifying in the antecedent that the subject is to consciously consider the question whether q—along with corresponding adjustments elsewhere in our argument.

Exclusion thus implies that in order to know full well that p, one must be able to "defend it in the arena of reflection": one must be able to view oneself as meeting every condition that one recognizes as required in order then to know that p; or, alternatively and to the same effect, one must be able to *exclude justifiedly* any possibility one consciously recognizes to be incompatible with one's then knowing that p.

Exclusion is a powerful principle in the skeptic's hands, once we are persuaded to grant the following:

> Here is something that most of us are fully justified in believing: that no belief can amount to knowledge unless formed in a way that is at least minimally reliable.

This fact in combination with Exclusion entails a "principle of the criterion":

> PC1. If one knows full well that p, while considering whether one knows that p, then one is justified in believing that one's belief that p is formed in a way that is at least minimally reliable.

Given how it has been derived, this we must still view as a principle about the contents of any given consciousness at any given time. Spelled out more fully, PC1 hence claims this: that if one consciously knows full well that p, and at the same time considers whether one knows that p, then one must be justified in believing that one forms one's belief in a way that is at least minimally reliable (that the source of one's belief is at least minimally reliable). Consciously knowing something full well while in the arena of reflection requires that one actively defend one's belief against all entertained possibilities that one consciously takes to be incompatible with one's knowing in so believing.

Undeniably there is much that one knows without being aware of it at the time. One still knows a lot when asleep and even when entirely unconscious. And we want our reflections to apply to knowledge generally, not only to the highly restricted domain of what rises to consciousness at any given time. Fortunately, we can broaden our scope with little or no loss in plausibility. We need only focus, not just on someone's conscious beliefs and experiences at the target time, not just on what they actually manage to defend reflectively; we need rather to focus, more generally, on what they *would* be able to defend, no holds barred, were it cast in the arena, perhaps by a hypothetical skeptic.

It would not do, however, to suppose that someone already knows something just because if they started thinking about how to defend their belief, they would *then* come up with a fine proof. Someone who guesses the answer to a complex addition problem does not already know the answer just because, given a little time, he could do the sum in his head. If he had not done the sum, if he had just been guessing, then he *acquires* his knowledge through reflection, and does not know beforehand. In some sense, at some level, if one already knows pre-reflectively, then the justifying reasoning must *already* be operative before one enters the arena. When challenged in the arena, one simply reveals the support that one's belief already enjoyed pre-entry. In order to occupy the desired pre-reflective position, moreover, one needs already, pre-reflectively, the wherewithal to defend one's belief if exposed to reflection, and one's belief must already be supported by the structure of reasons constituting that defense-at-the-ready. We are not just interested in the weaker position of someone who *would* be able to defend the belief, but only because its exposure to reflection would lead the subject to new arguments and reasonings that had never occurred to him, and that in any case had played no role in his acquisition or retention of the target belief.

Our most recent reflections in turn induce a second principle of the criterion:

> PC2. In order to know full well that p one must be justified in believing (at least implicitly or dispositionally, if not consciously) that one's belief that p is formed in a way that is at least minimally reliable, that it has an at least minimally reliable source (if the proposition that one's source is thus reliable is within one's grasp).

This principle is not restricted to beliefs entertained consciously; it is rather meant to apply more generally to implicit, subconscious, dispositional beliefs, and even to beliefs that one has while asleep or unconscious.

In fact PC1 and PC2 are only two members of a whole family of "principles of the criterion," whose unifying thread is that they all concern the satisfaction of requirements for various degrees of knowledge. Thus, certain levels of knowledge would be compatible with one's knowing the sources of one's belief to be just minimally reliable, but higher degrees would require knowing them to be quite reliable, or highly reliable, and so on.

B. The Pyrrhonian Problematic

Sometimes a justified belief is justified because supported by reasons; reasons that the believer not only *could* have but *does* have. The fact that given time one could think of some good reasons for believing something is not enough to make one justified in so believing. Again, someone who guesses on a sum could perhaps do the addition in his head; but, even supposing he *could* do it, that alone does not justify him in believing his guess before he actually does it. One's rationale for a belief cannot be successful if dependent on some arbitrary or otherwise unjustified component. Justifying beliefs need to be justified in turn. And now we have three possibilities. As we consider the reasons for one's belief, and the reasons, if any, for these reasons, and the reasons, if any, for these in turn, and so on, either (1) some ultimate reasons are justified noninferentially, are justified in some way that does not require the support of some ulterior reasons, or (2) there are no ultimate reasons: further reasons always justify one's reasons, at every level, no matter how remote the level, and these further reasons always go beyond any reason already invoked at earlier levels, or (3) there are no ultimate reasons: further reasons always justify one's reasons, at every level, but these further reasons need not go beyond reasons already invoked at earlier levels.

Possibility (1) corresponds to foundationalism. The foundations are constituted by the ultimate reasons that require no further supporting reasons in their own behalf. Possibility (2) is that of infinitism. Each supporting line of reasons extends infinitely to further reasons, ever-new reasons for the reasons at each level, no matter how remote that level may be from the justified conclusion. Possibility (3), finally, is that of the circle. One's justifying structure of reasons circles: some reason for a reason at a given level returns us to an earlier level.

C. Is foundationalism a myth?

According to conventional wisdom, foundationalism has been historically the option of choice. This, we are told, may be seen with special prominence in Aristotle among the ancients, and in Descartes among the moderns. According to this story, it is only with Hegel that persistent reflection on the ancient problematic yields a powerful defense of the circle. It took Hegel's philosophic genius to overcome the foundationalist inertia of the tradition and the immense influence of Descartes. Only Hegel returns to the ancient problematic and reveals the power of its anti-foundationalist side, and the virtues of circularity.

Among analytic philosophers, it is Sellars who took the lead against foundations, with his attack on the "Myth of the Given." The attack targets not just a givenism of sensory experience, but a much more general doctrine, one amounting to foundationalism of whatever stripe. Thus, Sellars's attack in "Empiricism and the Philosophy of Mind," focuses, not on experiential foundations via introspection, but on perceptual foundations via observation. The following is marshaled effectively in his critique of direct realism:

In order to be fully justified, perceptual belief requires background beliefs (assumptions) that in turn require justification.

In accepting the deliverances of one's senses one assumes that they are so constituted, and so adjusted to the relevant environment, that they tend to get it right.

More recently, Laurence BonJour has generalized from Sellars's principle as follows:

No belief B is fully justified simply because it satisfies some condition F such that beliefs satisfying F are probably true. The believer must *also* be aware, at some level, that B satisfies the condition.

This generalization, BonJour's Generalization, sets up a clash of intuitions. On one side are the epistemic internalists, who believe that justification requires justifying beliefs, and that no one can be really justified in a certain belief while unaware of its sources.

Foundationalism and its Myth of the Given were thus attacked famously by Sellars, in a way generalized by BonJour. But the sort of problem raised is not unique to their critique. A main theme of Richard Rorty's attack on foundationalism is the alleged "confusion of causation with justification" that he attributes to Locke and others. Donald Davidson also adds his voice: "As Rorty has put it, 'nothing counts as justification unless by reference to what we already accept, and there is no way to get outside our beliefs and our language so as to find some test other than coherence.' About this I am, as you see, in agreement with Rorty."[4] Just how damaging is that line of objection against experiential foundations?

Here intuitions clash. For externalists, a belief is justified by being related appropriately to its subject matter, perhaps causally or counterfactually, or by deriving from a reliable source that yields mostly true beliefs with great reliability. This need not come to the attention of the believer; it need only be in fact true, whether believed or not. On this side are arrayed Goldman, Nozick, Plantinga, and Unger, among others.

Intuitions in this stand-off have hardened over the years, and each camp tends to regard the other as just missing the point in some crucial respect.

---

[4] "A Coherence Theory of Truth and Knowledge," in *Kant oder Hegel?*, ed. Dieter Henrich (Stuttgart: Klett-Cotta, 1983), reprinted in Ernest LePore, *Truth and Interpretation* (Oxford: Blackwell, 1986), pp. 307–20; p. 310.

Most interesting for us is the fact that BonJour's Generalization (of Sellars's insight) is a member of our family of principles of the criterion.[5] So it should be as plausible as the two simple principles from which the family derives: namely, Ascent and Transfer. One reaction to this is to accept the Sellarsian reasoning and reject foundationalism. But if we reject foundationalism, then we are still caught in the Pyrrhonian Problematic. What then is the way out?

Ironically, a way out is opened already by the foundationalist-in-chief of the received story, Descartes himself, whose real view of these matters is quite subtle, or so I will argue, and must be approached gradually.

D. Descartes' way out

Three commitments are standardly attributed to Descartes, not all of which could be held by anyone of middling intelligence. The first doctrine is a rationalist foundationalism according to which "intuition and deduction are the most secure routes to knowledge, and the mind should admit no others." On this view, whatever one knows one must either intuit directly, through its immediate clarity and distinctness, or one must prove it deductively, on the basis of ultimate premises each of which is itself intuited as clear and distinct.

---

[5] This means that it can be traced back to our two simple basic principles, Ascent and Transfer, and that it has behind it the plausibility of these principles and of their supportive guiding ideas: (a) that knowledge is a matter of degree, and (b) that the epistemic level of one's knowledge is determined by how it connects with our objective of attaining the truth and avoiding error, and of doing so within a mind well enough integrated to attain not just truth but understanding, and thus the ability to answer the whys that voice our desire to understand.

According to the second commitment, in order to attain really certain knowledge of anything whatsoever, one must first prove that there is a God who is no deceiver. Consider, for just one example, the following passage, from the last sentence of the fourth paragraph of Meditation Three, where, speaking of the "metaphysical" doubt that he has raised, Descartes has this to say: "[I]n order to be able altogether to remove it, I must inquire whether there is a God as soon as the occasion presents itself; and if I find that there is a God, I must also inquire whether he may be a deceiver; for without a knowledge of these two truths I do not see that I can ever be certain of anything."

Descartes also apparently believes, third and finally, that God's existence and nondeceiving nature must be demonstrated through appropriate reasoning (involving, among other lines of argument, the ontological and the cosmological).

Clearly, these three commitments cannot be combined coherently. But the second and third would be hard to defeat, given their textual support. This puts in doubt the long and widely held belief that Descartes was a foundationalist.

On the other hand, the attribution of foundationalism to Descartes is not just arbitrary. There is textual evidence in its favor, including the passage above. Weightier evidence yet supports attributing to Descartes the second and third commitments, however, so that, if a foundationalist at all, Descartes was no simple or flat-out foundationalist. His position must be subtle enough to sustain not only the first commitment, under some interpretation, but also the second and the third. Consider a key passage in which Descartes claims epistemic advantage over the atheist:

The fact that an atheist can be "clearly aware that the three angles of a triangle are equal to two right angles" is something I do not dispute. But I maintain that this awareness of his [*cognitionem*] is not true knowledge [*scientia*], since no act of awareness that can be rendered doubtful seems fit to be called knowledge [*scientia*]. Now since we are supposing that this individual is an atheist, he cannot be certain that he is not being deceived on matters which seem to him to be very evident (as I fully explained). And although this doubt may not occur to him, it can still crop up if someone else raises the point or if he looks into the matter himself. So he will never be free of this doubt until he acknowledges that God exists.[6]

Here Descartes is not claiming only *ex post facto* advantage over the atheist. Take the moment when both are clearly and distinctly perceiving the fact that the three angles are equal to two right ones. *Even at that very moment*, according to Descartes, the atheist is at an epistemic disadvantage.

That, moreover, is not the only passage where Descartes claims or implies the specified sort of advantage. Here is another, from the last paragraph of Meditation Five (and compare also the fourth paragraph from the end of that Meditation):

And so I very clearly recognize that the certainty and truth of all knowledge depends alone on the knowledge of the true God, in so much that, before I knew Him, I could not have a perfect knowledge of any other thing.

---

[6] This passage is from the Second Set of Replies as it appears in *The Philosophical Writings of Descartes*, ed. J. Cottingham, R. Stoothoff, and D. Murdoch (Cambridge: Cambridge University Press, 1985), vol. II, p. 101. Where this (CSM) translation says that an atheist can be "clearly aware," Descartes' Latin is *clare cognoscere*.

According to this, *cognitio* of the true God is required for *scientia* of anything whatever.

Descartes was well aware of the Pyrrhonian Problematic, as may be seen, for one example, in his "Search for Truth." Such skepticism suffused his intellectual milieu, and he knew its content and sources. Against this backdrop, a passage from Sextus is revealing:

Let us imagine that some people are looking for gold in a dark room full of treasures.... [N]one of them will be persuaded that he has hit upon the gold even if he *has* in fact hit upon it. In the same way, the crowd of philosophers has come into the world, as into a vast house, in search of truth. But it is reasonable that the man who grasps the truth should doubt whether he has been successful.[7]

No one is likely to disdain the good fortune of finding gold in the dark. On normal assumptions, one is of course better off for having done so. More admirable yet is getting the gold through one's own efforts, however, where one succeeds through one's own deliberation and planning. Here success is not just luck in the dark; it crowns rather an enlightened pursuit of a desirable goal. In that passage Sextus suggests distinguishing similarly in epistemology. Here again it is more admirable to attain one's worthy objective through one's own thought and efforts than it is to be a passive recipient of brute luck. At a minimum it is better to proceed in the light of an adequate perspective on one's own cognitive doings.

If convinced by this Pyrrhonian thought, Descartes *would* make just the distinction he does make between *cognitio*

---

[7] *Against the Mathematicians*, VII. 52, in the Teubner text, ed. H. Mutschmann (Leipzig, 1914).

and *scientia*. *Cognitio* is the attaining of the truth, which can happen through one or more layers of good luck, in the environment, in oneself, and in the adjustment between the two. One might of course attain the truth through luck, by a mere guess that the fair dice will come up seven, and surely this does not yet qualify as *cognitio*. *Cognitio* requires at a minimum that one attain the truth by being appropriately constituted, and appropriately situated, to issue reliable judgments on the subject matter. So constituted and situated, one *would* be right on that question. Here of course are matters of degree: how reliable are one's operative dispositions, one's epistemic competences? Are they infallible? Nearly infallible? Very highly reliable? And so on. This has to do with how easily one might go wrong in thinking as one does through exercising the relevant dispositions, one's faculties or virtues. *Cognitio* furthermore requires that the correctness of one's belief be attributable to the exercise of such a competence in its appropriate conditions. *Cognitio* is animal knowledge, or apt belief.

Scientia requires more. It is attained only through an adequate perspective on one's epistemic doings. Only if one can see how it is that one is acquiring or sustaining the belief in question does one attain *scientia*. What is more, one must see that way as reliable, as one that would tend to lead one aright, not astray. But this is just what is required by our principles of the criterion. According to this family of principles, various levels of knowledge will require various degrees of perceived reliability in the sources of the belief constitutive of the knowledge. In accepting Sextus' Pyrrhonian thought, therefore, Descartes would be accepting the importance of satisfying a principle of the criterion, whereby one must believe one's source to be reliable. How reliable? This will depend on how high a level of knowledge is selected in the context.

Suppose Descartes accepts the Pyrrhonian Problematic, and accepts also Sextus' contrast between attainments in the dark and those that are enlightened. In that case he faces this question: is enlightened knowledge possible for us? Can we attain an enlightened perspective on what we believe and on our ways of acquiring and sustaining those beliefs, one that reveals the sufficient reliability of those ways? This, I submit, is what sets up Descartes' epistemological project. He is trying to meet Sextus' demands, to the extent that these are reasonable. Further features peculiar to Descartes' own project derive from his desire not just for reasonable and reliable belief but for absolutely certain and infallible knowledge. However, much of interest in his thought need not be tied to that desire.

In a bare sketch, here is how I see Descartes's epistemic project. First he meditates along, with the kind of epistemic justification and even "certainty" that might be found in an atheist mathematician's reasonings, one deprived of a world view wherein the universe may be seen as epistemically propitious. Descartes' reasoning at that stage *can* be evaluated, of course, just as can an atheist mathematician's reasoning. Atheist mathematicians will differ in the worth of their mathematical reasonings. Absent an appropriate world view, however, no such reasoning can rise above the level of *cognitio*. If we persist in such reasoning, nevertheless, enough pieces may eventually come together into a view of ourselves and our place in the universe that is sufficiently comprehensive and coherent to raise us above the level of mere *cognitio* and into the realm of higher, reflective, enlightened knowledge, or *scientia*. No circle vitiates this project.[8]

A mere thermometer reaction to one's environment cannot constitute real knowledge, regardless of whether that reaction is causally mediated by experience. It is not enough that one respond to seeing white and round objects in good light with a "belief" or "proto-belief" that one faces something white and round. Having asked oneself "Do I know that this is white and round?" or "Am I justified in taking this to be white and round?" suppose one has to answer "Definitely not" or even "Who knows? Maybe I do know, maybe I don't; maybe I'm justified, maybe I'm not." In that case one *automatically* falls short, one has attained only some lesser epistemic status, and not any "real, or enlightened, or reflective" knowledge. Knowing *full well* thus requires some awareness of the status of one's belief, some ability to answer that one does know or that one is epistemically justified, and some ability to defend this through the reliability of one's relevant competence exercised in its appropriate conditions. But this leads to a threat of

---

[8] In order to raise one's belief that p above the level of *cognitio*, to the level of *scientia*, one may well need appropriate *cognitio that* one enjoys *cognitio* that p. I have heard the objection that comprehensiveness and coherence are matters of degree while it is very hard to see how to draw a line above which lie the degrees of comprehensiveness and coherence that suffice for knowledge. But compare a concept like that of being tall. That is presumably to be defined in some such way as this: being sufficiently taller than the average. Presumably someone just infinitesimally taller than the average is *not* tall. One has to be taller than the average by some margin, one has to be "sufficiently" taller than the average. But how do we define that margin? Is there, even in principle, some way to capture our *actual* concept of tallness by means of some such definition? There seems no way. Yet we do surely have and use a concept of tallness, do we not? Why can't we view epistemic justification similarly in terms of "sufficient" comprehensiveness and coherence?

circle or regress, a main problematic, perhaps *the* main problematic of epistemology. Surprisingly, already in Descartes himself, the founder of modern epistemology,[9] we find a way beyond it.[10]

[9] Many others since Descartes have groped for a similar way: from Hegel through Sellars. Much work on epistemic circularity has also appeared of late, and some of it is discussed in my "Philosophical Scepticism and Epistemic Circularity," *Proceedings of the Aristotelian Society*, suppl. 68 (1994): 268–90. In "How to Resolve the Pyrrhonian Problematic: A Lesson from Descartes," *Philosophical Studies* LXXXV (1997): 229–49, I argue more fully that Descartes shows us the way beyond that problematic; and in "Mythology of the Given," *History of Philosophy Quarterly* 14 (1997): 275–86, I argue for the relevance of that bi-level solution to the problematic of the given, which is present in analytic philosophy from its earliest years. My forthcoming *Virtuous Circles: Apt Belief and Reflective Knowledge, Volume Two* (Oxford: Oxford University Press, 2007) is devoted to issues of epistemic circularity.

[10] I have earlier presented the ideas in this chapter in several venues and am grateful for helpful formal comments by Laurence BonJour, Peter Klein, and Richard Fumerton (respectively at an APA symposium, the Chapel Hill Colloquium, and the Oberlin Colloquium).

Appendix

This will address further issues that I aim to clarify for concerned readers. (Here we enter subtleties that might have proved distracting to auditors.)

I

Against the proposed virtue epistemology, it might be objected as follows:

> Both the kaleidoscope perceiver and the ordinary perceiver, in taking themselves to believe aptly, must depend essentially on a false presupposition. They both must presuppose that their experience would not then mislead them, a false presupposition in each instance. Even the ordinary perceiver, when he self-attributes an apt perceptual belief, must presuppose that this perceptual belief would not then be false if based on a corresponding sensory deliverance. And no belief that is based essentially on a false presupposition can possibly amount to knowledge.

Or so goes the objection under review. But why, exactly, must the meta-competence of the ordinary perceiver work through the false presupposition that the deliverance of his color vision *would not then be false*? Only thus, it may be thought, would he be able to sustain his meta-belief that his object-level perceptual belief is apt, given principle C.[1]

That objection misconceives what principle C requires, however, what it requires for the correctness of a belief (or an apprehension, presumption, etc.) to be attributable to an epistemic competence. The relevant epistemic competence here is a disposition to accept the deliverances of an epistemic source, and a source is itself a disposition to host certain intellectual seemings in appropriate conditions. If the disposition to accept these deliverances is to constitute an epistemic competence, the source must be truth-reliable enough in its deliverances, *when in its appropriate conditions.* According to principle C, moreover, the correctness of a belief is attributable to an epistemic competence only if the exercise of that competence *in its appropriate conditions* would then yield a correct belief. And this does not require for perceptual knowledge that the deliverances of the perceiver's relevant senses would not then be misleading. It is required only that they would not then be misleading if delivered *in its appropriate conditions.*

The ordinary perceiver need not presuppose that a deliverance of his senses *would not* then mislead him. The most he need presuppose is that the deliverance *would* not mislead him *so long as the conditions were appropriately normal.* Abstracting from the appropriate normalcy of the conditions, the most he need presuppose is the material conditional that if he is offered that deliverance then it is a true deliverance.

---

[1] For convenience, here now is that principle:

C. For any correct belief that p, the correctness of that belief is attributable to a competence only if it derives from the exercise of that competence in appropriate conditions for its exercise, and that exercise in those conditions would not then too easily have issued a false belief.

This is the most that is essentially involved in competently accepting the deliverance of his senses at face value. And *this* presupposition, being a material conditional, can well be true, and by hypothesis *is* true, both in the case of the kaleidoscope perceiver and in that of the ordinary perceiver. However, only the ordinary perceiver can *aptly* believe this material conditional; the kaleidoscope perceiver is precluded from doing so by the presence of the jokester.

We first moved from a requirement of sensitivity to a requirement of safety. Even this requirement turned out to be too strong, however, since a belief can fall short of safety in ways that do not deprive it of the status of knowledge, either animal or reflective. A belief can be unsafe through dangers to the relevant competence of the believer, or to the conditions appropriate for its exercise. And neither of these dangers would take away the aptness of a belief that gets it right through the exercise of that endangered competence in its endangered conditions. Moreover, an apt belief can even be aptly believed to be apt, and hence amount to knowledge that is not only animal but also reflective. This aptness-centered account enables a solution not only to the problem of radical skepticism, but also to the more difficult problem of dream skepticism. But the competence that most fully accounts for our being right, when we are, is very often socially seated, by comparison with the constitutive subcompetence seated in us individually when we receive testimony at the end of a testimonial chain.

II

One interesting question remains: can an apt unsafe belief amount to reflective knowledge? Or must we still require safety for reflective knowledge even if it is not required for animal knowledge? Well, if the orthodox conception of dreams is correct, then our ordinary perceptual beliefs are unsafe but still apt, and aptly believed to be apt. They are unsafe because too easily we might have believed falsely in believing as we do, either through impaired competence or through degraded conditions, since we might too easily have been dreaming in so believing. Despite this lack of safety, however, if in an ordinary case of perception we do use a normal perceptual competence in its normal conditions, then our belief is apt and qualifies as perceptual animal knowledge. Moreover, as we have seen, such apt belief can also be aptly believed or presumed to be apt. Safety is not required, therefore, in a belief that constitutes reflective knowledge by being aptly believed or presumed to be apt. On the orthodox conception of dreams, ordinary perceptual beliefs are not safe, but they are still apt, and aptly believed or presumed to be apt.

III

How do we distinguish the conditions that are "appropriately normal"? This distinction is plausibly part of a package that includes the concept of an epistemic source, and the competence/incompetence and success/failure distinctions. Derivatively from these, we have also the distinction between apt and inapt performance. A competence is a condition on the part of an agent whose manifestations are successful performances, when in appropriately normal circumstances. An apt performance is one that is successful because competent. A performance can fall short of success, in which case, trivially, it would also fail to be apt. But it might still be competent, so long as it fails only because of the bad circumstances.

What then makes circumstances appropriately normal? This is of course a relative matter. Circumstances might be normal with respect to performances and competences of one sort, while abnormal with respect to those of another sort. They might be normal for pistol shooting while abnormal for archery (too much wind). Or they might be normal for the use of our eyes but not our ears. And so on. The appropriate normality of circumstances for performances of a certain sort depends on normal human competences, on normal human abilities to attain some sort of thing of value, or at least valued, in certain sorts of circumstances, within certain parameters, such that it is of interest to us whether or not someone does have the ability to succeed within the relevant parameters. So, we seem to determine competence/circumstance pairs, such that an agent's ability is a state that he is in, whose deliverances would tend to be successful, in conditions within the relevant parameters.

That sort of conceptualization is not restricted to the realm of human competences or virtues. What makes a temperature thermostat a good thermostat, for example, is its ability to perform well, to hold the ambient temperature within certain bounds, provided the circumstances are appropriate for its operation. For a thermostat, this requires that it be properly installed, properly connected to a furnace, perhaps. The fact that the thermostat fails when disconnected is not relevant to whether it is a good thermostat. Nor is it relevant to its performing well that it might very easily have been disconnected. Its performance at that time need not have been safe outright, then, in order for it to have been apt, and attributable to the quality of that thermostat. Nor is it relevant that someone might easily have disabled it by pouring glue into its inner workings, someone in the wings who had the motivation and opportunity. The fact that either possibility might easily enough have occurred would make the thermostat's performance unsafe: to the extent to which either might easily have occurred, to that extent is the device's performance one that might easily have failed. (I am here assuming that in at least some examples the performance would have been individually the same performance despite the impaired competence of the performing instrument.) However, neither threat would undermine the aptness of the thermostat's performance. Suppose that it might very easily have been disabled (by the glue), or out of position for proper operation (by being disconnected); nevertheless, so long as it was *actually* in working order, and normally connected, the device's performance is apt even if unsafe, and creditable to it as its doing.

IV

When we take experience at face value, are we not *thereby* in a state with its own propositional content? Are we not assessable epistemically for having such a disposition in terms of the truth of some such propositional content? Well, what might that propositional content be? Is it that whenever, wherever we seem to see a red surface, we do see a red surface? Is this what we are implicitly committed to in trusting our color vision in that instance? No, that cannot be right. Surely we can know that to be false, without this affecting our competence and our continued rational use of it in specific instances. Perhaps we should view the content required not as a general proposition but as something like a propositional schema, or perhaps we should view it as a "generic" proposition to the effect that such appearances are veridical, or perhaps as a "tendency" proposition to the effect that such appearances tend to be veridical.

In any case, when we manifest our general disposition in a specific instance, we go beyond any such schematic, generic, or tendency proposition, to commitment about how matters stand in that instance specifically. So, what content might our specific commitment have, when we do in that instance accept the deliverance of our color vision? Might it be some such implicit content as the following?

That one's color vision would not then deliver an appearance as of a seen red surface unless one did then see a red surface.

If this is a commitment constitutive of the kaleidoscope perceiver's exercise of his color vision, however, then we lose our defense of his animal knowledge, and with it our solution to the problem of dreams. For, it will not be plausible to claim the following three things in combination about that perceiver:

(i) that his belief rationally requires his commitment to the claim that his color vision would not deceive him in that instance;
(ii) that this commitment is in fact false, given the jokester in control;
(iii) that in spite of (i) and (ii) the perceiver knows the seen surface to be red.

However, it is far from clear why perceivers who enjoy perceptual competence must make such strong commitments. Why not understand differently their implicit trust in the deliverances of their senses? Why not require only an implicit presupposition with *material* conditional content, or one that takes the form of a schema, or of a generic, or tendency proposition? The default competence exercised by someone gifted with color vision might then implicitly take it for granted that if something seems to be red, then it is red (and so on), where the conditional involved is only material.[2]

---

[2] If it is thought that conditionals in normal use, even indicative ones, are rarely if ever material, then the ordinary perceiver's presupposition might better be, not *that if it seems red then it is red*, but rather the likes of this: *that it does not seem red without being red*.

Index